GOLFING WITH THE ENLIGHTENED DEAD

Lessons on leadership and meaning from the pros

D.C. Malloy
&
D.L. Lang

PNEUMA SPRINGS PUBLISHING UK

First Published in 2016 by:
Pneuma Springs Publishing

Golfing with the Enlightened Dead - ***Lessons on leadership and meaning from the pros***

ISBN13: 9781782284079

British Library Cataloguing in Publication Data. A catalogue record for this book is available from the British Library.

Cover art work credit:
The Enlightened
(Mixed media collage 5x7)
by Laurie Kilgour-Walsh 2015

Photography by Kyle McLeown

Edited by Richard Hovey, Associate Professor, McGill University, Montreal, Canada.

Pneuma Springs Publishing
A Subsidiary of Pneuma Springs Ltd.
7 Groveherst Road, Dartford Kent, DA1 5JD.
E: admin@pneumasprings.co.uk
W: www.pneumasprings.co.uk

Dedication

This book is dedicated to Group Captain DG Malloy DFC. A decorated fighter pilot, an outstanding athlete but most importantly a brilliant husband and father. Cheers Bud!

Praise for

Golfing with the Enlightened Dead - Lessons on leadership and meaning from the pros
by D.C. Malloy & D.L. Lang

"This is truly a fascinating book. It makes the ideas of the great philosophers meaningful to everyday life. A remarkable achievement."

- Dale Eisler, Senior Policy Fellow, Johnson-Shoyama Graduate School of Public Policy, Former Assistant Deputy Minister, Natural Resources Canada & Consul General to the USA

"It's very accessible. Over nine holes of golf we are introduced to the ideas of some of the great thinkers and shown how we can all become applied philosophers, using these ideas to lead better lives. The world needs more applied philosophers!"

- Elizabeth Fistein PhD MRCPsych
Ethics and Law Lead, School of Clinical Medicine, University of Cambridge

"What if you could play a round of golf with history's most provocative philosophers? The Enlightened Dead gives us that opportunity and at the same time offers a practical guide to leadership. A great read for fans of golf, leadership and philosophy."

- Bryan Walkey
President, MeetingZone North America

"This book offers meaningful insights from Socrates, Aristotle and other great minds to help give you a "competitive and meaningful advantage" in today's business world.

Dave Ploughman President & CEO, BSTREET Group, Toronto, London, New York

"Play a round of golf ... and learn the origin of foundational theories of organizational behaviour."

Rob Cooke, Leadership Advisor and Strategist

Table of Contents

The Players: Sages and Lunatics

The Philosophers

Socrates – father of Western philosophy

Aristotle – father of Western science and logic

Heidegger – philosopher of time and thinking

Nietzsche – philosopher of passion and pain

Vivekananda – Hindu mystic of Karma-Yoga

Sartre – philosopher of freedom and responsibility

The Psychologists

Freud – father of psychoanalysis

Adler – father of will to power

Skinner – father of behaviourism

Frankl – founder of logotherapy

The Golfer

Bud Graland – former fighter pilot, student of leadership, "scratch" handicap, good listener

The Course – Somewhere in Scotland

PREFACE

While each of us has a sense of what the words leadership, work, and philosophy mean individually, we rarely see the three of them combined and put into action. This book is an attempt to show how leadership, work, and philosophy interrelate and how the great thinkers of the past might approach leadership today; it's an attempt to work through their particular intellectual lenses. Ordinarily such a discussion is difficult, complex, and far from a leisure activity, or it is portrayed much too simply, preventing you from establishing a strong philosophical foothold. In this book, we take you down a different path - through a quick round of golf, during which our characters discuss these ideas. Through golf, a remarkable and profoundly philosophical game, we contemplate happiness, joy, frustration, and despair. The game acts as a testing ground for our ability to deal with adversity when we hit a ball out of bounds twice off the tee, or three-putt a green, or want to toss our clubs into the pond after double-bogeying the eighteenth hole. It also brings out the very best in us when we graciously adhere to etiquette on the course or when we refuse to cheat by kicking a ball out of a bad lie in the rough even when we know we could get away with it. Golf acts as a midwife, helping deliver the best and/or worst in us.

Before we go any further, let's be clear what we mean by the term philosophy. At least three perspectives come to mind. First, we can certainly think of it as something professors do for a living - thinking of obscure ideas, writing their thoughts using complex often impenetrable jargon to their colleagues at other universities who are trained in the same complex language - a world of their own that sometimes makes little sense to the average person. Second, we can also think of philosophy as power. Why power? Because by thinking through everyday problems with different lens we are much better decision-makers. As better decision-makers we are more powerful and effective leaders. Finally, we can think of philosophy as a means to achieve a sense of meaning in our work, in our leadership, and in our lives. As such, philosophy can be viewed as a 'tool box' of ideas that we can use to build our lives moment by moment and decision by decision. The essential point to take from the latter two views is that philosophy should not be left only to those paid by universities. It should be embraced by any one of us with will to be curious, creative, and the desire to find meaning in what they do.

THE SCENE

We are joined in this round of golf by Bud Graland, a student of both golf and leadership, and by a mixed bag of sages and lunatics from the past. We hope that you enjoy the round and that this book will help you see leadership and work through new lenses. Perhaps it will even improve your game!

Bud had much on his mind and was desperately in need of a quick nine holes of golf to provide the context for some much-needed introspection. In his life, he had been a profoundly respected fellow, a gentleman and a decorated fighter pilot who loved the great game of golf. He had enjoyed a successful career in the Royal Air Force, and at age fifty-five, he had left the military to become a successful entrepreneur. As a consequence, he had experienced the world of work both as a senior leader in a large, complex, traditional, and highly structured bureaucracy – the military - and as an independent businessman whose success was fully dependent upon personal creativity in a culture of chaos. Bud was well acquainted with and completely fascinated by the many ways in which people approach work and leadership. He had, over the years, been an avid reader of organisational and leadership theory books. He was well versed in all the quick fix–checklist approaches and in the more academic psychological strategies to get people to work harder, better, and longer. But these pop-culture and academic approaches always left him wanting – there had to be something more!

Bud had recently accepted a vice-president position with the company he had been with for twenty-plus years. In his previous roles within this company, Bud had felt competent, confident, and comfortable. But now everything had changed; his new role carried significantly more responsibility and higher expectations. His worry and concern about this had resulted in many sleepless nights over the past few weeks, with no let-up in sight. The vice-president of human resources had thoughtfully offered to provide leadership training at a posh resort, but to Bud, the current theories seemed to be superficial attempts to hide organisational manipulation. He needed something more – something he could genuinely embrace as noble leadership.

There was a time when Bud believed that leadership was a formula, that if he followed it step by step or adopted "habits of highly effective leaders," leadership would be easy. Certainly these pop experts knew all the tricks to get the most out of people in a workplace – at least in the short term. But Bud had been sent to these leadership courses and sessions before, and upon reflecting on those experiences, he realized that these courses and seminars reminded him of quick-fix fitness gimmicks and self-help books. None of which work because they avoid deeper issues such as self-perception, emotional states, and stress.

Bud reflected on all of the self-help books he had read over the years; like most diets, these books suggest the possibility of change but are too superficial to be profoundly helpful. Could a week in "leadership boot camp" be enough to help Bud achieve the depth and quality of leadership that he hoped to bring to his new job? Leadership by numbers, the tips and tricks of leadership, a mythological approach to dealing with people: how could they help over the long term?

At that moment, Bud recalled a friend's reaction to his worrying. She had put it simply: "When you are ready, a teacher will appear." At the time, Bud had dismissed this as being somewhat Star Wars-ish and fluffy - certainly not something he could use. But as he recalled the countless times when chance meetings with people (teachers) had helped to clear up confusion or lead him down another path, his friend's words began to resonate. Perhaps he needed to be more open to the possibility of meeting those teachers, to learn to listen, to be fully present while in conversation, and to ask for help.

Bud's mind was soon filled with possibilities and projections of what he needed to understand to confront his sense of discomfort. As humans, we try wholeheartedly to avoid discomfort even though it tells us much about ourselves - what we need to learn and how to move forward. He realized that a quick fix would not be enough to enable him to be the authentically tuned-in leader he wanted to be. The answers to his questions would emerge from deep and meaningful conversation with people who had thought deeply about the essence of being human, about leadership and being-in-the-world. But where were these teachers and how was he going to find them?

One day in June, the weather was as nasty as any British Open could offer. The wind was howling, rain was pelting down, and the temperature was dropping - the best place to be was at home in front of a fire reading a good book. Yet Bud and his son Brian, who was always up for an adventure, decided to brave the elements and go out for at least a quick nine holes. They arrived at the course dressed for a typhoon, walked to the first tee, and braced themselves for a challenge.

As always, Bud suggested that his son hit first. Brian, an excellent golfer, took his usual graceful swing, but because of the rain and a wet grip, the club head turned in his hand on his downswing resulting in the ball flying off the club at a forty-five–degree angle toward a large oak tree and then rebounding back like a squash ball, hitting his father square in the forehead. Down he went, like a boxer on the losing end of a left hook. Bud opened his eyes to bright sunlight, stood up, and found himself still on the first tee. The rain was gone and so was his son. He looked around at the familiar sights of his favourite golf course and thought to himself, everything seems different - it's the same landscape but the colours are brighter, the sights and sounds clearer. Then he met his first dead enlightened golfer …

The First Hole
Socrates and the Midwife

Leadership is midwifery. Pull what you can from individuals' minds by asking questions. Individuals then become aware of their abilities to be engaged and to take pride in their work.

– – – – –

The first hole is a reasonably straightforward 373-yard par four with a green that is guarded by a "burn" (a Scottish euphemism for a death-by-water hazard).

A short bald man with a scruffy beard, and clothes that appeared to have been slept in was standing on the first tee, seemingly in a trance as he stared down the fairway. Bud approached him and extended his hand in greeting. No response. "Good morning. Would you mind if I joined you today?" No response. Then another golfer came up beside them and whispered that Socrates often did this when a dilemma perplexed him; people simply have to play around him when he is deep in thought. Bud took a closer look. Yes, he now saw the resemblance to a bust that he had in his office, picked up in a market in Athens many years before - the same snub nose and large protruding eyes. He waited a few minutes as the previous group made its way down the first hole. Suddenly Socrates shook himself and murmured, "Yes, definitely a 5 wood, slight draw into the wind, then a three-quarter swing with a seven iron. The ball will land on the right side of the green and roll down to the left within ten or twelve feet. One putt - birdie - perfect."

Bud stood back, impressed with the imaging and sheer intensity of concentration that this strange fellow had just demonstrated. But would theory translate into action? Socrates stepped up to the ball and, like the cartoon version of the Tasmanian devil, swung hard, pounding his ball straight out of bounds. He teed up a second ball and swung mightily again: the ball skipped off the end of the tee box. Strangely, Socrates seemed totally unaffected by these mishaps. He carefully replaced his 5 wood in his bag and, after waiting while Bud effortlessly drove his ball slightly left of centre to avoid out-of-bounds on the right side, they started walking. Bud couldn't help but notice the seeming discrepancy between the intense strategising before the first swing and the actual technique and outcome; he had to ask Socrates about it. The response was dignified yet curt: "Theory is perfect, humans are fallible."

As they proceeded down the first hole, with Socrates eventually making the green after five shots (plus his 2 stroke penalty) and Bud landing safely on his second swing, he asked Socrates what it was like being the world's most famous philosopher. "Actually, I always thought of myself more as a midwife of ideas," was his reply. Bud, who was not trained in philosophy or in midwifery, pressed him for details; he was, as usual, more than happy to accommodate.

Midwifery and Giving Birth to Ideas

Socrates. Philosophers are lovers of wisdom. Of course, they love the knowledge, beauty, and truth they discover themselves, but some also feel a calling to help others become philosophers, or at least philosophical in their daily decisions. They do this because they believe that of all of the components of being human, it is our capacity to reason - to think logically through problems - that makes us uniquely capable of good and evil. If we could only be more philosophical, more truth seeking … just wiser … we would have better tools to construct and maintain the "good life."

Now personally, I believe that pure forms of knowledge of all things exist within us, though I know that this is not a terribly modern perspective. Nonetheless, I believe that they reside in our souls from birth. In other words, we have the capacity to know truth in all of its forms if only we are able to tap into our souls. This is obviously easier said than done because we often don't know what questions to ask ourselves to get this information out to the conscious level – we need help to do this. Unfortunately, most of us never receive this kind of help; rather, we are told what to do, and how, when, and sometimes why to do it – our parents, teachers, coaches, and bosses leap in to guide and control so that we behave obediently and according to what society and organisations dictate. This is the "mind is a blank slate" notion made so popular about two thousand years after my death by two fellows named John Locke and Thomas Hobbes. They believed that we know nothing when we are born – we are not pregnant with ideas – and therefore we must have our minds filled by those who do know things.

In contrast, I believe that the mind is not empty, but profoundly full of ideas waiting to emerge – waiting to be born. Whether or not you actually believe that the soul contains these truths isn't the point; what is important is that we all have ideas. Many of them are profoundly practical and some are deeply philosophical, and the leader's task is to help us bring these ideas to the light of day.

For example, in one of Plato's dialogues, the *Meno*[1], he wrote about me having a conversation with an uneducated slave to demonstrate that we have innate, or inborn, knowledge. During this conversation, despite the fact that this fellow had had no formal training in geometry, he was able to arrive at Pythagoras' theorem by responding to the questions I had carefully selected for him. What Plato was getting at here is that regardless of what hidden knowledge one is trying to extract from a pupil, if you ask the right questions, he or she will arrive at or give birth to the correct answer eventually and will feel empowered by doing so. The opposite approach, of course, would have been to tell the slave about the theorem and hope for a successful regurgitation, possibly with little or no understanding. Does this approach sound familiar – like contemporary teaching strategies used from kindergarten to university?

As you can see then, my perspective is that the job of the philosopher is to act as a midwife, helping individuals to give birth to and become aware of ideas they already have so that those ideas can be used to live well. This simple process has been called the Socratic method of teaching.

Bud. Okay, Socrates, fair enough, but let's put this into a narrower scope – leadership and work in a twenty-first-century organisation. How does the idea of midwifery emerge in the leadership context?

[1] It is important to note that Socrates never wrote anything with regard to his philosophy. Most of what we know about him is the result of Plato featuring Socrates as the main character in most of his dialogues or philosophical plays. As a consequence, it is difficult to distinguish between the philosophical ideas of the two men.

Socrates. Plato, my student, danced around this idea of mine in another one of his dialogues that he called the *Sophist.* Here he described the ideal teacher or, in this case, the leader as a therapist of the soul. Essentially, what he and I were getting at is that there are two ways to teach or lead. One is through telling the student exactly what to do and think. The other is to question and challenge the individual thoroughly in order to remove unfounded opinion and to reveal truth unencumbered by hearsay or opinion.

Put into an organisational context, rather than telling employees what to do and expecting them to follow because they are being paid to do so, the ideal leader will empower employees to resolve a given dilemma, not by telling but by questioning them and thus leading them toward self-discovery. Let me ask you, my dear Bud, what would be the advantage of self-discovery and empowerment?

Bud. Well, if nothing else, it would make the whole enterprise of work dramatically different. Individuals would presumably take more interest and pride in their work because it would, in fact, be *their* work as opposed to simply doing the bidding of others. This sounds wonderful in theory, but what about the demands in terms of time that this would take? It's much easier and efficient in the short term to simply tell the employee what to do, tell the soldier when to fire, tell the student what to memorize ...

Socrates. Yes, this is true in the short term, of course. But in the long term – the life of the employee, the life cycle of the organisation – it may be well worth the effort for leaders to take the time to establish rapport, to dialogue with and build faith in employees. Take the scenario of a newly appointed manager. For argument's sake, let's say that this individual, Linda, is a well-trained and well-educated employee. On her first day on the job, Linda is instructed by her new boss simply to watch and listen to how the job is done. This shadowing continues for a week - a bit long in Linda's mind, but she's new and still learning the ropes. During her second week, the senior manager allows Linda to perform only the most menial tasks; this becomes rather frustrating for her since she feels more than qualified and capable of being fully engaged. Finally, after a month, Linda is "let loose," but her every move is carefully watched - every e-mail is proofread, every telephone conversation with clients is in a conference mode with her boss, and any deviation from organisational norms, let alone standing policy, is quickly pointed out and corrected.

Linda is being micro-managed, cloned into the image of the senior manager and stifled as a contributing employee, and as a person. All of this is done under the assumption that only the organisation, through its most senior managers, knows what is best; the lower echelons are to be force-marched to follow, regardless of what they may have to offer. This is efficient in the short run because it maintains the status quo of the system and the working system must be perpetuated. It is also efficient if the employee is willing to be perceived as a tool - an empty vessel willing to be filled by others. But if we are more than simply tools for the organisation's use and if we have our own creative ideas to offer, even within the context of structured bureaucracies, then such an environment will eventually lead to dissatisfied employees whose sense of authenticity has been compromised. The outcome: loss of employee commitment, high turnover and absenteeism rates, sabotage - and ultimately long-term inefficiencies.

But there is much more at stake than long-term efficiency. Successful work, particularly in the last hundred years, has been based upon three cardinal virtues - productivity, efficiency, and effectiveness. The legitimisation of these virtues is based on our almost unquenchable thirst for technology and bureaucracy. In order to satisfy this thirst, empowerment and pride of the individual worker has been lost. It reminds me of the legend of Thermopylae. Remember that the Persians failed in their invasion of Greece in part because their troops were mercenaries, fighting for gold and not meaning. The devoted and victorious Spartans, on the other hand, fought to save their homeland and their families' lives - what could be more meaningful and noble?

One could say that the problem with our concept of work today is that we, as leaders, have failed to make work a medium for self-discovery and meaning. Sadly, we have instead fashioned it to be a mercenary task, which slowly eats away at our core until we cry out in a midlife crisis or we succumb to the death of our authentic selves and to the meaninglessness of work.[2]

Bud. Hold on, let me try to take this in smaller bits. You are suggesting, then, that leadership facilitates self-discovery. Leaders can do this not by telling individuals what to do, filling the empty vessel, but by pulling what they can offer out of them - finding out what they know instead of assuming they know nothing.

[2]Authenticity is a term used extensively in philosophy (particularly existentialism) as a descriptor of the individual who refuses to assume the roles that family, the organisation, and/or society expects him to play. Authentic or genuine individuals are true to themselves and accept responsibility for this genuineness. The inauthentic individual takes on the persona that is expected, despite its incongruence with the true self. For example, the graduate from an MBA program who chooses to use her skills to feed the poor rather than pursuing the Fortune 500 career may be expressing a rejection of expected social role-playing in favour of an authentic expression of self.

Socrates. Yes, that's it.

Bud. Okay, let me keep going, I'm on a roll. Leaders can also make work something more than simply the means to make money or the means to finding meaning once work is over - right? In other words, they can avoid the Persian error. Work in itself can be meaningful each day if there is a leader to help each employee through the self-discovery process. And let's take this one step further: a leader could also establish a culture for this to become an expected outcome of working in this particular organisation. Is that what you're getting at?

Socrates. Well, yes. There is even more to it than this, but that will have to wait for the ninth hole. In the meantime, think of it this way. Self-discovery is a way of tapping into one's potential, and as you will find out on the next hole, reaching our potential is our utmost concern. While the ideal - pure knowledge through self-discovery - is certainly the target that I strive for, some would argue for a reasonable balance because, after all, we live in a real world that tends to throw us into the rough or out of bounds every now and then.

Bud. Do you mean balance in terms of reasonable expectations of work, meaning, making a living, dealing with crazy co-workers …

Socrates. It's time you met one of the best of Plato's students - the best despite the fact that he disagreed with most of what I said!

Socrates three-putted for a ten, and Bud, who had floated a wedge beautifully, high up over the burn, two-putted for par. After replacing the pin, he turned around to walk to the next tee. Socrates was nowhere to be seen.

Relevance of Socrates

While so much of what Socrates said (that is, what Plato wrote) may at first glance have precious little to do with the twenty-first century and even less to do with leadership and work, deeper scrutiny reveals valuable and practical knowledge.

Of the many Socratic ideas we could have discussed, we chose to superimpose his theory of knowledge on the concept of leadership. The Socratic method benefits leaders by maximizing input from subordinates: the greatest leadership error is assuming that followers know nothing.

Socrates argued that what we know is what we have recollected. By this he meant that we do not really *learn* anything – rather, we *remember* and our memory is stimulated by a competent mentor. His theory goes something like this: the knowledge that we can "access" is housed in our soul, which has been not only reincarnated but also in contact with perfect knowledge (if ever so briefly) before landing in our bodies. As we discussed earlier, our task is one of pulling out knowledge rather than filling up an empty vessel or blank intellectual slate. Regardless of whether one believes Socrates' notions of reincarnation or innate knowledge, the point that we can "extract" from this is that we all have valuable knowledge of many things, but often we do not have the courage to voice our perspectives for fear of being wrong, or of being rejected, or of being noticed. It is not uncommon for leaders to fail to recognize this knowledge due to their fear of being upstaged or the belief that a "subordinate" with less experience and/or fewer credentials simply would not be able to contribute without being given a directive – "Your job is not to think but to follow orders."

But if you are a leader who is not intimidated by staff input and if your goal is employee fulfillment and the betterment of the organisation, then the role of midwifery using the Socratic method to extract latent knowledge from employees is for you. Essentially what we are saying is this:

- everyone in the organisation has something worthwhile to offer over and above merely following orders;
- not everyone is going to willingly offer his or her perspective without a climate of trust, creativity, and freedom; and
- as a leader, you can function as a midwife.

So how does one do this? *Socratic method* is the term for the question-and-answer style of "teaching" used by the midwife. Rather than minutely directing tasks to be performed, the midwife asks pointed questions to enable individuals to freely voice their views and discover that they can indeed make valuable contributions toward the overall success of the organisation. This may in turn result in a sense of empowerment and an enhanced perception that work, regardless of what it is, can be an outlet for creativity.

The approach can be as simple as asking employees probing questions about what they think the resolution to a problem might be or asking them what the organisation could be doing better and taking the feedback to heart. It can also be as complex as asking questions that may lead to a refined sense of the organisation's key principles (for example, respect in the workplace) in the same systemic way as Socrates probed the slave in *Meno*.

The Driving Range: Putting Theory into Practice

How can you as a leader put Socrates' ideas into action? Give your employees - actually, everyone around you - some credit for either knowing something or having the ability to discover it for themselves. Individuals will have a greater sense of ownership of their decisions and will feel more empowered to take on leadership roles within the organisation. The bottom line - it instills confidence, always a good thing, and it is your job to pull this confidence out of your employees!

The Next Tee...

Success in golf is related to restraint - some would call it temperance. Too much technical thinking distracts the golfer from the flow of his swing; too little thinking results in stupid shots. Too much power results in the golfer losing control of her swing; too little power makes the goal of parring the occasional hole rather unattainable. The right amount of thinking and the right amount of power and technique results in "virtuous" golf. On the second hole, Bud and Plato's student, Aristotle, discuss virtue and how virtuous living (and golf) leads to what Aristotle calls <u>eudaimonia</u> - which is the target (or flag) at which we should aim.

The Second Hole
Aristotle and the Target for Living Well

The goal of living is happiness; the target of happiness is to flourish. We can do this through work – if it is balanced. Balance implies that one objective of work is to develop a deeper understanding of oneself. The leader's role is to ensure that this objective can be reached in each person's organisational role, regardless of what it is.

– – – – –

The second hole is a par four, 453 yards of fear. You can barely see the fairway from where you tee off, and there are bunkers and gorse to the right and a great bloody wall to the left that runs down the length of the hole. Even if you survive the first shot, you still face the approach to the green, which is equally nasty.

On the second tee, Bud found a rather distinguished-looking fellow waiting for him. Impeccably dressed (in a toga), he was surrounded by a small crowd who appeared to be hanging on his every word, which was occasionally accented by a slight lisp. Bud approached the tee, and immediately Aristotle offered his hand in a warm greeting and introduced himself – though his face needed no introduction. He explained that the crowd were his students and that rather than sit in a lecture theatre, it was their habit to go for a walk and discuss philosophy. Today they found themselves at the golf course. Graciously, Bud suggested that Aristotle tee off first. The latter considered his driver and then thought perhaps this would take him too close to the wall; he started to pull his four iron out of the bag but then realized that this might fly him into the hidden bunkers two hundred yards out. Three iron! Not too far, not too short. The crowd applauded Aristotle's drive, though they had no idea where the ball had landed. Bud hit his driver. And off went the peripatetic golfers.[3]

As Aristotle and Bud walked down the second fairway, the followers attended to the philosopher's words as if they were a dictum from God. The throng seemed a bit out of place in the middle of the fairway, though, and Bud gently requested that they line the side of the rough, in case the philosopher missed the fairway on his next shot. Once the followers moved on, Bud remarked that

"I just played the first hole with the teacher of your teacher, Plato. Socrates is quite an interesting character to say the least."

Looking slightly annoyed, Aristotle said, "I know, I saw him and was desperately trying to avoid him. I can't cross the street without him trying to get into some grand debate about truth as being found only in perfect ideas or concepts as opposed to the physical world of sense perception - Plato is the same ... they never stop."

"Well, what do *you* think?" asked Bud.

"Frankly I think it's both, but that's a discussion for another day. What I find much more practical are discussions about living the good life."

The Good Life

Aristotle. Consider for a moment the kind of life, in the broadest terms, that you could live. A life focussed on

[3]The term peripatetic was used to describe Aristotle's habit of going for more intimate philosophical walks with his favoured students as opposed to his public lectures in Athens. It literally means "the ones walking about."

seeking physical enjoyment or pleasure? A life centred on gaining and maintaining power? A life given to reflection or contemplation? And before you answer, consider the strengths and weaknesses of each.

Bud. All right. At first glance, a life of physical pleasure or enjoyment sounds wonderful, but I can see that over time, this would become unfulfilling. I don't think that "sex, drugs, and rock 'n' roll" sustains you when other capacities for growth are left unattended – like having a family, for example.

Aristotle. I agree, and I'd take this one step further. In itself, physical pleasure is fine, but focussing on it reduces the human to the level of a non-rational animal. This kind of life prevents you from reaching your potential as a human. I have referred to this in my lectures on ethics as a focus on *apparent* goods as opposed to *real* goods. The former concerns things that seem to provide us with happiness but in fact take us away from our proper goal; the latter concerns those activities that do, in fact, lead toward true happiness – but here we are getting a bit ahead of ourselves. What about the second kind of life?

Bud. I think a life centred on seeking power can also be viewed as positive, at least in limited doses. To rise to the top of your field, to gain control over yourself and your environment, is a goal that we all take on at a young age and is something to which many of us aspire. And to gain respect and status among your peers is also a welcome feeling. Having said that, I suppose it is possible that over time the appeal of having status may wane – like a rock star being surrounded by fans. It's initially a desirable situation, but eventually it becomes an intolerable one. George Harrison hated being a Beatle after a few years of over-the-top adoration by people who didn't really know him at all.

Aristotle. Agreed. The life of power - or as I have called it, "the life of the statesman" - is perhaps more laudable than the life of enjoyment, but it still doesn't appeal to the highest calling of the human as a rational being. Furthermore, it requires others to honour you: it is not self-sufficient because you need them.

Bud. Well, that leaves me with the life of contemplation. The weakness? Let's see. On the surface, most people would see this life as difficult, lonely, and boring, and sadly, many would argue it's not practical. Similarly, in the conversation I had with Socrates earlier, we discussed how our contemporary world has become so focussed on technology - the "what" and the "how" - and we seem to have forgotten about thinking or contemplating the "why." The outcome of this focus on outcome has been modern society's race to achieve unsustainable wealth using unsustainable resources at the cost of the unhappiness of those who cannot keep up with this race to 'development' and 'progress'. So although we pay little attention to the life of contemplation it may, in the end, be the most important life to lead.

Aristotle. Yes, this is what I believe. And it's also the key to living a life of true happiness, or as I would prefer to call it, *eudaimonia*. This word encompasses what is in my opinion the ultimate aim of human activity - to flourish. Because we are rational animals, we can only reach our potential - that is, flourish and self-actualize - if we engage this capacity for reason. To seek physical pleasure and/or social accolades alone will lead to an unfulfilled life... in the end.

Now, it would be unreasonable to suggest that one should therefore give up physical pleasure or should not seek acceptance in one's social milieu. I am not suggesting that we should all become hermits in caves staring at our navels in apparent contemplation. Not at all. We need to have fun because we are social as well as intellectual animals. But our failure has been and continues to be the lack of value we place on our contemplative or meditative capacities. Ideally and practically, we need to live a life of balance - that is, a life of virtue.

Bud. Yes, Socrates thought you would say this to me. Too much contemplation may be, in this day and age, as unbalanced as too little. I mean, we do have to eat and we do have to perform tasks that are sometimes unpleasant in order to feed ourselves and our families. But I suspect you're going to say that this is to be expected in the real world - as opposed to the Platonic ideal world.

Aristotle. Very good, Bud. You seem to have a good grasp on this debate I've been having with Socrates and Plato for the past two millennia. I suspect we'll still be arguing about it two millennia from now as well. So let's move on and discuss how we get to our intended target.

My perspective is that we can flourish if and only if we live virtuously. To me, virtuous living implies that one is striving to avoid excess and deficit in all activities - with the exception of wisdom, justice, and perhaps noble love. For example, based upon my metabolism, I should eat a certain amount of food to keep me healthy - this would be different, of course, for an Olympian. If I eat excessively, I will gain unnecessary weight; if I eat too little, my health will also suffer. Virtuous eating is the mean between excess and deficit for me. Let's take another related example - investments. A portfolio with too much money invested in risky stocks and none in bonds is financially dangerous. By the same token, too much invested in safe bonds and little in the more volatile stock market will not result in a fruitful, or virtuous, portfolio. The best strategy is to have a blended balance of stocks and bonds.

Aristotle's ball had landed out about 213 yards, very close to the wall. He had a five wood and nine iron to go. Bud's ball had ended up about 190 yards away from the pin - reachable with a four iron. The next shots would be very tough, as the green had a bit of slope to it.

Bud. Okay, I'd say your main points so far are these:

1. A life of contemplation is needed but often overlooked.

2. The goal of human life is to flourish and we need to exercise our rational capacity - contemplation - to achieve this.

3. We can flourish by avoiding excess and deficit in all of our activities.

Am I right?

Aristotle. Clearly you missed your calling as a philosopher - please go on.

Bud. Okay. Now my interest, apart from playing this silly game of golf, is contemplating the idea of work and leadership. If the goal in life is to flourish, can I do this through work or does work only give me the resources to flourish on the weekend or in my retirement? Essentially what I am asking is, is it too much to ask that work be more than a financial means to an end?

Aristotle. That is an excellent point. Let me explain after I hit my ball.

He took his 5 wood and, not too quickly and not too slowly, swung and made square contact with his ball - which flew left to right with a slight fade directly into the burn. Aristotle's response appeared to be not too frustrated about a nice shot gone bad, yet not too optimistic about a par. Bud's 4 iron landed short of the green beside a bunker on the left - par was still within reach.

Aristotle. It's not inconceivable that one can flourish at work. But from my recent observations of work activity on earth, it appears that flourishing rarely happens, or if it does, that it's by chance and not a result of the system or the wise counsel of a manager or leader. It doesn't seem to be a priority as much as the rush to be efficient, effective, and productive.

Bud. I agree. It seems that so many work in order to live well when the workday is over, or they work for early retirement, or, the most fatalistic of all, they buy lottery tickets to escape from the meaninglessness of work, usually to exchange meaningless work with meaningless pleasure. We seem to be unaware of the potential for work to be a place where we can flourish. With more than a bit of frustration, I read through my son's organisational behaviour textbooks periodically, and nowhere is there a mention, let alone a chapter, on how to make work more than simply meaningless toil. Of course, there are theories that provide leaders with strategies to motivate employees to work harder - even to convince them that their personal goals are entwined with the organisation's goals - but these are ultimately strategies of manipulation. Genuine individual flourishing as a corporate responsibility doesn't even have a deaf ear to fall on because the idea is never spoken let alone contemplated. Vocation and *eudaimonia* are ships that pass each other rather silently in the night.

Aristotle fished his ball out of the burn and wedged it onto the green – it landed short of the pin but then rolled backward to the front fringe. Bud chipped his ball and left it short by about twelve feet. Two putts each, friendly applause from the peripatetics, and off they went to the third tee.

Relevance of Aristotle

Aristotle comes from a lineage unsurpassed in the history of ideas – preceded by Plato and Socrates. His work went far beyond the traditional realm of philosopher as we understand it today: he could arguably be called the father of science because his interests extended into biology, anatomy, physics, politics, and more. From Aristotle's work, we chose to focus on the notion of virtue and *eudaimonia,* his term for happiness or flourishing.

Aristotle's formula is simple. Live virtuously in a habitual way, have good fortune, and you will achieve happiness or *eudaimonia*. This needs some unpacking.

Virtue is achieved when you choose between excess and deficit – the *golden mean*. For example, you should not work too much or too little, eat too much or too little, exercise too much or too little – rather, always choose the middle path. Learn to do this habitually – it must become part of your lifestyle to choose not too much or too little of anything (except wisdom and justice, according to Aristotle). But choosing the middle path is not enough. You must also have good fortune, and this depends on your family and friends, your community, and, in our context, your workplace, which must be one that allows you to live, act, and decide virtuously. The combination of "golden mean" choices and good fortune results in a human being who has flourished, who has achieved happiness and self-actualization. Stated another way, virtuous behaviour results in a life that has reached its potential - and this is the purpose of life, to reach one's potential physically, socially, and, most importantly (according to Aristotle), intellectually.

The value in this for the individual is clear, but what is the connection to leadership and work? One may argue that it is the leader's role to create an environment that will, at least in the context of work, result in good fortune. In other words, the leader creates an organisational culture that enables the follower to choose virtue over vice and the middle path over excess and deficit. For example, the virtuous organisation does not foster workaholism or pressure to make a short-term sale where one needs to "cheat" a customer. Rather, the virtuous organisation supports balance in work and family, as well as balance between profit and social responsibility. Such an organisation holds the long-term view that success, or organisational flourishing, is not reached through one sale or one act but through a lifetime of wise decisions.

Virtue in the workplace is possible but not probable in today's business environment. Aristotle gives us the route for virtuous work: maximize the potential that exists within us, for our own well-being and especially for those with whom we interact. The probability of achieving this is unlikely because leadership training programs, both formal and informal, emphasize goal achievement at all costs. One does not have to ponder long on the calibre of virtue inherent in Ponzi schemes, or in the leadership that contributed to the financial meltdown of 2008. There is no virtue here.

But the business world does not have to be this way. In truth, Aristotle might single out many well-known businesses as evidence of virtuous leadership. The Bill and Lynda Gates Foundation easily comes to mind, but the teamwork of Milton Milken and Nobel Laureate Mohamed Yunus, although lesser known, may have even greater significance for guiding young business entrepreneurs in virtuous business practices.

The Driving Range: Putting Theory into Practice

Aristotle argues that a life well lived is about more than just money and status (a point we will return to later). Rather, a happy life is one that allows the individual to flourish or self-actualize. We all know this implicitly but when it comes to reward and punishment in the workplace, it's all about the money. It's odd that we still don't place greater emphasis on self-actualizing and implicit motivation when all of the research suggests that this leads to more intense commitment among employees. Aristotle was right 2,300 years ago - and he's still right today, yet we don't seem to get it. So what to do? Be sure that basic needs are satisfied - good pay, good working conditions - and after that find out what would lead to an environment in which employees could flourish. How can you help them find themselves and develop as individuals? Begin by asking them what is and/or could be fulfilling in their working life and go from there!

The Next Tee...

The obvious goal of the game of golf is to hit the fewest number of shots possible. We tend to get rather upset when we exceed what we perceive to be our maximum allowable number. In fact, some of us get so focussed on the number that we lose sight of the reason why we play the game in the first place – a case of not seeing the forest for the trees or cursing a beautiful sunset because it is obscuring your vision of the pin. Martin Heidegger, a twentieth-century German philosopher, felt that the "modern" individual has forgotten how to see the big picture altogether. Had he been a golfer, he certainly would have scoffed at our obsession with the score card, as well as our obsession with materialism and our flight from meditative thinking. Bud encounters Professor Heidegger on the next tee.

The Third Hole
Heidegger and the Lost Art of Meditative Thinking

To fully understand any decision we are about to make, we must be able to think both calculatively and meditatively. Leaders must know the forest and the trees intimately.

— — — — —

The third hole is another par four, 397 yards long. The fairway is wide open but lacks a flat landing area. You could blast off a driver without much fear of trouble, with the exception of an old cart path well right of the rough. A decent tee shot would give you a short wedge to the green.

Silence greeted Bud on the next tee. The peripatetics had vanished, and sitting quietly on a bench was a very serious-looking man with a thin moustache. As Bud approached, the gentleman jumped to his feet and, with an elegant movement, offered his hand and at the same time bowed slightly, cocking his head to the right. He introduced himself with a slight German accent as Professor Doctor Martin Heidegger and welcomed Bud to the 3rd tee. Bud shook his hand and began surveying the fairway. Both men proceeded to hit their drivers: the exacting Dr. Heidegger was straight down the centre, while the more aggressive ex-pilot hit his ball with a bit of a draw, landing slightly in the rough about seventy-five yards ahead of the German professor.

Bud. Well, Professor, what brings you out here on such a fine day?

Heidegger. It has been my custom to seclude myself as much as possible when I am thinking, and at this time of day, the course is usually empty - with today's exception of Aristotle's gang, who are always unruly. Their beer consumption always seems to exceed their master's golden mean!

Bud. What is it that you're thinking about?

Heidegger. Actually, I think a great deal about thinking. Two kinds of thinking to be specific: calculative and meditative. I find that we do far too much of the former and have forgotten completely how to do the latter. Let me explain.

Calculative thinking involves the what, how, where, and when of any action or behaviour, past, present, or future. It is the thinking of science and engineering in their purest technological sense. This kind of thinking perceives most objects - such as nature, for example - exclusively as a resource for exploitation. Taken too far, it results in humans treating other humans as means to ends rather than ends in themselves.

Bud. Could you explain what you mean? I think an example might help me understand.

Heidegger. Yes, of course, Herr Graland. Let me give you a few examples, if I may. When the coach, the team, or even the nation perceives the athlete as a machine trained to win medals and not as an athlete-as-person, we have calculative thinking. When this athlete fails or is injured, he or she is quickly replaced by a faster, stronger, healthier model, without a second thought. Likewise, a worker occupies a role that has been designed by someone else in order to create an effective, efficient, and productive organisational "machine." Individuals become cogs in wheels and are replaced when they break or become inefficient. There is no emotion, compassion, introspection, or meaning attached to the sport or to the factory toil - humans are treated with the same dignity, or lack thereof, as non-humans and mechanical parts.

In the realm of science, a defining moment in calculative thinking was the development of the nuclear bomb by Robert Oppenheimer during the Second World War. This scientist was given a task by the U.S. government and he created this weapon, presumably to show that he could do it - a technological puzzle to be solved. However, once he realized its horrific potential for destruction after the test in July 1945 at Los Alamos, New Mexico, he quickly reversed his support and became a vocal critic. One might argue that while he was able to meet the challenge of "how," he failed, until much later, to address the challenge of "why."

Allow me to give you another example. You may recall that in the 1960s the Ford motor car company created a model called the Pinto. This car was known to be defective and could explode upon collision, yet Ford did nothing to protect its customers. Why? Well, a cost–benefit calculation suggested that to do nothing would cost the company less money than to recall and repair the automobiles (Shaw & Barry 1989). The creation of the nuclear bomb and the decision by Ford are both clear examples of calculative thinking.

Bud watched as Heidegger carefully surveyed the sloping green, trying to decide between a nine iron short to avoid a downhill putt or an eight with some backspin, hoping for a generous roll toward the flag. Prudently, he hit the nine and landed on the front edge of the green: a twenty-foot putt for birdie lay in waiting. Bud walked toward his ball, knowing a wedge would do the trick. He executed a beautiful swing, with the club head forcefully driving down and through the ball, sending it skyward up and over the bunker that guarded the pin. Unbelievably, the ball hit the flag and careened straight across the green into the opposite bunker. He looked over to Heidegger, who bowed and clicked his heels. In need of consolation, Bud asked the professor to explain the meditative mode of thinking.

Heidegger. Meditative thinking does not imply meditation in a Zen-like manner. Rather, it implies pondering the so-called big scheme of things as the backdrop against a single event or situation. For example, an athlete is injured perhaps a concussion and the coach doesn't think that the team can win without her. So does the coach put the player back into the game, risking permanent injury to win a particular game? In the calculative mode of thinking, this is a real possibility. With meditative thinking, the athlete and coach will place this particular game against the backdrop of the potential for a lifetime of disability and choose wisely to pull the player from the contest. Should a parent scold a child for spilling milk accidentally? In the grand scheme of life's events, is this really an issue worthy of raised voices and punishment? Is the exploitation of nature for the immediate economic benefit of this society or this generation acceptable against the backdrop of environmental degradation for other societies and future generations? If and only if we use this forgotten capacity of ours to think in a reflective manner, considering the broader meaning of our actions, the answer to all these questions is clearly "no." But this capacity for meditative thinking is a lost art, and we have only ourselves to blame. This is the way we teach our children to think – science without philosophy or meaning. Just because we can, though, doesn't mean we should.

Bud. Well, let me throw this idea out: can you say the same thing about a career against the backdrop or horizon of a life well lived?

Heidegger. Yes, Herr Graland, that is exactly my point. A career lived calculatively is a career lived in pursuit of material wealth and social power; it is not a career lived with meaning. The outcome is superficial work-as-toil without an awareness of the deeper purpose that it may have, regardless of what kind of work you do. Now if we addressed the meditative aspect of work, we could perhaps identify its deeper meaning – that which makes it worthwhile apart from acquiring money, security, and corner offices. For example, how often do executives walk down the hallway and compliment the janitor for all of the hard work he does to make the building look clean and vibrant? Does the student serving coffee at the corner café hear a word of thanks from customers or realize herself how important that first cup of coffee is to so many people in getting their day started? What kind of day would we have if these two individuals failed to do their jobs? In my own experience as a professor, I believe that universities would cease to exist without coffee being readily available.

Now please don't misunderstand my intention here. I am not suggesting that we do away with calculative thinking. That would, as Aristotle would say, place us out of a virtuous balance. If we did forego calculative thinking – as we have with meditative thinking – then we could certainly never finish a round of golf, let

> alone organize ourselves into virtuous organisations or hold well-structured board meetings. What I am suggesting is that in order to make sense or meaning out of what we do with our lives, we need to revisit the meditative mode of thinking as a way to balance it with technology.

Bud exploded out of the trap to within three feet of the cup and tapped in to remain even par after three holes. Heidegger's long birdie putt rimmed the cup, and he finished with a four. Against the horizon of the back nine holes, he realized that one par does not make a good round of golf ... but it helps. Noticing the trend of the last three holes, Bud wondered who would be there to greet him on the fourth hole - the most difficult of the front nine.

Relevance of Heidegger

The idea of Heidegger's work being applicable to real life may seem to some to be almost comical, as his academic writing style makes his work virtually impenetrable. But despite his perhaps vainglorious attempt to over-intellectualize, some gems have sadly been left to obscurity, not the least of which is his distinction between meditative and calculative thinking. As children of logic and the scientific method, we are well versed in the latter. We have been trained to be empirical animals praying at the altar of quantitative data to establish our truth. Our philosophical focus, particularly in North America, has been the problem-solving approach of pragmatism, which has left us intellectually barren of any thought beyond the functional.

Heidegger's message to us is to open our awareness to what exists holistically rather than to focus exclusively on the specific. In addition to our narrow gaze on the accomplishment of specific goals and objectives, we need to broaden our view to include the wider implications of our actions. A specific decision may solve an immediate problem, but it may also create a cascade of problems unforeseen by the calculative eye. This broadened view is related to the capacity to think in a meditative or reflective way.

Case in point: we are aware of our job descriptions, yet we are likely unaware of our mission or vision. This is partly due to the fact that visions and missions are rarely taken seriously, even by those who create them – they are generally perceived to be corporate rhetoric. While this certainly does not hold for all organisations, it may well hold for most. Part of the problem is that we know we should consider vision, but due to the calculative orientation in our school systems and workplaces, we are unable to do anything with vision – we do not make use of our capacity for meditative thinking.

The stock market crash of 2008 is a classic example of short-term gain without any consideration for long-term sustainability. It was predictable, but the calculative mindset of the stock market culture led to a profoundly narrow horizon, with the dangerous additives of greed and hubris.

What is the meditative role for the leader? It ties in neatly with the Socratic midwife role and the Aristotelian search for happiness. The Heideggerian leader will ask employees or followers to think beyond the immediate and the obvious. He or she will ask them to expand their intellectual and decision-making landscapes and consider that which will lead to a more comprehensive outcome. In addition to extending the intellectual capacities of the employees, this allows them to see how their work contributes to something beyond their immediate tasks and beyond themselves and this in turn imbues work with meaning. How important is the server at the local coffee shop? If we were unable to buy our morning cup of coffee, where would we all be? She may have no idea how important she is!

Another valuable contribution for leadership from Heidegger is found through understanding the perspective that nothing happens outside of personal contexts. This means that within the workplace, an individual will interpret and translate each occurrence into an action, response, or behaviour based on how that occurrence directly or indirectly influences that individual. Knowing that human beings behave this way helps us to understand, forgive, and hopefully modify not only the decisions we make but also how we implement them.

The Driving Range: Putting Theory into Practice

Heidegger argues that we are in flight from meditative thinking. In other words, we have become so enthralled by what we *can* do that we have lost touch with what we *ought to* do - we just don't see the big picture. Christopher Hodgkinson (1996) points out that this is the difference between management and administration or leadership. It is the role of the leader to be visionary, to see the big picture and to ensure that all calculative efforts are directed toward that end. Heidegger clarifies the important distinction between two ways of thinking and allows us to choose the appropriate thinking for each situation. At least now we see that there is a choice.

The Next Tee...

There is no doubt that golf causes most of us a fair bit of pain, warranted or not. Interestingly, most of us go to great lengths to avoid this pain or to rationalize it away. The wind took your ball out of bounds (it's not your fault that you sliced it badly) or the greens keeper cut the grass too short (it isn't your fault for three-putting). There is one philosopher who would do anything but *alleviate your suffering because he believes that what doesn't kill you makes you stronger. Without pain and passion, we are incomplete humans; thus we need to embrace our agony over lost golf balls and "shanked" wedges. Friedrich Nietzsche meets Bud on the next hole and opens up the welcome notion of passion and pain in the world of organisations*

.

The Fourth Hole
Nietzsche, Pain, and Passion

Self-awareness can only come about when one pushes the limits of one's ability. Pain is not to be avoided but to be welcomed in the same way that a well-exercised muscle must break down before it can be made stronger.

— — — — —

The 480-yard par four is by far the most treacherous hole, as a peninsula of scrub grass extends into the middle of the fairway. Golfers have to decide whether it's best to play safe and hit short off the tee or to attempt to fly this hazard without going too far and rolling into a fairway bunker. A big drive would still leave you with a long second shot into a nasty green sloping left to right with a rather deep bunker that has the potential to swallow the golfer whole.

Bud strolled up to the tee and found, waiting impatiently, a slight man with a very large moustache that could have been mistaken for a small broom. The two men exchanged greetings and prepared to tee off. There was never any doubt how Nietzsche would play the hole - he selected his driver and aimed for the thin slice of fairway along the right side of the hole. If he missed, he would be in grave trouble, but if he made it, he would have an ideal approach to the green. He teed his ball and with an unorthodox swing, faded it in a beautiful arch to the perfect spot on the fairway. Bud was most impressed. This fellow took the game seriously and dangerously. Bud chose to hit cautiously to the left side of the fairway, where there was a larger landing area but a more difficult approach to the pin – the ball rolled into some gorse. His prospects looked bad.

Nietzsche. This fourth hole makes me feel so alive.

Bud, biting his lip at the irony of this coming from a dead philosopher. Really. Looking at my lie in the gorse makes me feel like hell.

Nietzsche. Well, perhaps had you taken a more risky shot, you would have at least felt somewhat exhilarated at your failure.

Bud. Yes, but this is a difficult hole. I thought it best to play safe.

Nietzsche. Well, my friend, playing safe is in fact the problem, not only with this silly game but with life in general. Golf takes the passion out of one's soul because it forces us to be careful, to be intellectual and unemotional. It's a game in which we must analyze each and every movement to avoid danger, and as a consequence, there is no passion. Life in the Western world has become the same. We live carefully, we work inspired by security and benefits, and if we are lucky enough, we might experience a touch of passion accidentally, but certainly not because of the society of which we are a part. This capacity for passion we have indeed forgotten, and one of the culprits is the organisation.

Bud. Fascinating … please tell me more. But first, what do you mean by passion?

Nietzsche. Passion is our drive to create. It is our will to become who we choose to be. It is our excitement in expressing ourselves physically and conceptually. It is this passion that has been snuffed out of us so that we will be calm and obedient members of the organisation, culture, society, and congregation.

Bud. How has work, or the organisation, caused the loss of passion? And by the way, isn't this a good thing in terms of efficiency?

Nietzsche. Work has been passionless for most people since the Industrial Revolution. Marx called it alienation – the separation of the individual from his or her craft. For example, the cabinetmaker used to make the whole cabinet and presumably took great pride in this creative act. But this was perceived to be inefficient because it was much faster and economical for one person to make only knobs, another only doors, another only hinges, and then have someone else put it all together without the other contributors seeing the final product. The advantage: efficient, effective, and productive cabinet output with secure employment. The disadvantage was the individual's loss of pride in creating unique crafts and seeing them through to completion – or birth, as that nasty man Socrates would say. So work was no longer an expression of individuality and authentic creativity, but a means to an end – money. This was further exacerbated by bureaucracies that placed each individual in a particular role with particular expectations. The individual's personal values and, without a doubt, their passions for creativity were not to be revealed during working hours. So there you have it – bureaucracy and the death of passion.

Bud. This sounds a bit extreme, but I can see where you're going with it. Bureaucracy is here to stay, though, because, for better or worse, we are institutional beings now – we can't get away from being organized in one way or another. That being said, is it inevitable that we will continue to be passionless?

Nietzsche. So your question is, are societies or organisations in which passion is valued possible? Only if people are willing to suffer.

Bud. Okay, now I'm confused. Why do I need to suffer?

Nietzsche. Suffering is needed in order to overcome our own inertia of complacency. For example, I can play this game of golf safely – never taking a chance, never fully expressing myself. As a result, I will hit the ball a mediocre length and get a mediocre score. Or I can attempt difficult shots, experience failure, and try again and again until I achieve a higher level of ability, a more complex understanding of myself. Let's look at the world of the entrepreneur. Have you heard of Ed Mirvish, or "Honest Ed" – Canada's self-proclaimed inventor of the loss leader?

Bud. Yes, I have. Actually, I've had a steak at his restaurant in downtown Toronto.

Nietzsche. Well, Mr. Mirvish began his working life at fifteen in order to support his mother and two siblings after his father died at a young age. Ed ran the family grocery store, which he then turned into a dry cleaner. During World War II, he and his wife opened a dress shop, and then, following the war's end, he used his wife's life insurance policy to open up a bargain basement using the 'loss leader'[4] as the driving strategy. The rest is history. Honest Ed's brought in millions and Mr. Mirvish became an extremely

---

[4] A loss leader is a tactic to draw in customers by introducing the sale of an item well below cost with the hope that consumers will buy additional items at regular mark up once they are in the store.

wealthy businessman and philanthropist, as well as a recipient of the Order of Canada and a Commander in the Order of the British Empire. How did he do all of this from a teenager running a failing family grocery store? He accomplished this because of his passion and willingness to face danger - economic danger. I would contend Bud that only when I engage in something in which I know I may suffer can I find true passion. Without the expression of my passion for golf or philosophy or work, I am incomplete.

Bud. Mirvish's story is a great one, and I suspect, not atypical of many entrepreneurs worldwide who have overcome outrageous odds to reach success. But this may be easier said than done for those who are not independent business people. Are workers who are part of a bureaucracy doomed? In other words, while organisation and passion seem to be incompatible, I wonder if it may be possible to instil a sense of passion, or creativity within organisations. In my conversation with Socrates on the first hole, he pointed out the difference between two methods of teaching and learning. The first is based upon self-discovery, with the leader pulling ideas from the individual, asking such things as "How do you think you should approach this task?" The second is the forced regurgitation of information given to the individual by the leader - that is, telling the individual, "Do the job this way!" The latter is the typical mode of operation in a bureaucracy and likely does not result in a passionate environment. The former, it seems, would create an environment that would foster passion in one's work. It would present individuals with the possibility of succeeding if their ideas led to solutions. It may also present the possibility of failure if these ideas were not adequate -

forcing further examination, exploration, and introspection.

Nietzsche. Yes, definitely. The potential for death when climbing a mountain, for a lost golf ball when shooting for the green, for the failure of a risky business venture or an attempt to solve an organisational problem will inspire passion and breathe life into one's existence.

Nietzsche's ball was perfectly placed in the narrow landing area on the left side of the fairway. An easy 5 iron could have him putting for birdie. Bud, on the other hand, was in some trouble. He managed to find his ball in the gorse, but hitting out of this was impossible. He took a drop with the penalty. Nietzsche swung first and hooked his ball far left of the green – at least a half wedge to get back. Bud hit a six iron to the back of the green – a long putt ahead but he was out of the gorse and, because of his prudence, he did feel a lack of passion for the next putt. Nietzsche ventured off the fairway to find his ball and Bud proceeded to the green. Nietzsche, whose vision was obscured by the mist that had just blown over the course, miscalculated his approach and landed short. He two-putted for a bogey. Bud three-putted and silently wondered if he should have tried for the green on his second shot. But it seemed to him that perhaps Nietzsche had taken this notion of passion and pain too far – he seemed unhappy, even miserable, though what he said about pushing oneself to self-discovery did make sense. Bud was again reminded of Aristotle's belief in the *golden mean*: we shouldn't lose control of our passion, but neither should we become automatons. There must be a middle path to follow that allows us to express ourselves yet at the same time not lose our ability to reason.

Relevance of Nietzsche

Nietzsche represents us all in many ways. He is as much psychologist as philosopher, and through these perspectives, he tells leaders that to fulfill our essence - our authentic existence - as humans we must recognise and release our passion in all aspects of our life. Leaders must demonstrate passion and arguably must encourage those around them to be passionate and authentic about their work.

To allow ourselves to live in this way, Nietzsche implores us not to simply accept the status quo as given to us by religion, culture, or society, but to search for what is real and true for the individual. Not unlike Freud, who implores us to cast off our childish beliefs about God as an old man with a white beard who will take care of us, Nietzsche wants us not only to think for ourselves but also to moralize for ourselves – to find our own sense of good and evil. In *Beyond Good and Evil* (1973), he describes how the weak, by sheer number, are able to convince the noble that their pursuit of strength, power, and vitality was in fact evil or even sinful. In place of these "noble" characteristics, the weak - en masse - promoted the values of acceptance, democracy, empathy, sympathy, and so on in order to promote and protect the weak, powerless, and impotent. While this raises an eyebrow in our current context, his message is to be truthful to ourselves, to be independent and authentic, despite the pain and difficulties that this may lead us toward.

Nietzsche, not unlike the Buddhist, viewed pain and sorrow as welcome friends who challenge us to become better. A "soft" unchallenged life is analogous to a muscle that is never stressed – it becomes atrophied and ultimately useless. In contrast, a difficult life, if it doesn't kill us, makes us stronger and may help us to fulfill our potential.

The Nietzschean leader, then, will not seek the status quo and will not avoid challenge. Rather he or she will seek out change and push individuals to their limits like a coach will push an athlete to perform at higher and higher levels. We can be complacent animals, avoiding change and staying within the safety of the herd. We can see change as an indictment of our work or as intimidating to our skill sets and our egos. But Nietzsche argues that we are also animals that feel pure delight when we overcome obstacles like taking our first step, breaking a hundred on the golf course, or learning a new software program.

Part of our lack of passion in work is that we rarely connect the two. Passion is left for our spouses, families, hobbies – and work is how we pay for them. Does it need to be this way? Can the leader pull passion out of the individual? Can work-passion be an undiscovered land that is found with the help of an insightful leader-midwife?

Leaders must access some key information about their followers before working toward inspiring passion:

- What do employees find exciting about work?
- What do they hate?
- What motivates them?
- What are they passionate about outside of work?

What is the common denominator for each individual, and how can this be infused into his or her role in the organisation?

The Driving Range: Putting Theory into Practice

Nietzsche is all about pain. More subtly, he's about pushing oneself and others to go beyond the normal range of effort into a realm that may result in great joy or great sorrow. The goal, of course, is an authentic awareness of who you are, which is achieved by exploring your limits. Placed in the context of work, it is the leader's role not only to push himself or herself past the norm but also to expect and encourage employees to flee from mediocrity as fast as they can … for their own good.

The Next Tee…

Golf, like all sport, is a game geared toward an outcome. The goal is to play eighteen holes in the fewest strokes possible. Because the game is broken down into eighteen separate units, the challenge is always to keep one's head when one of these holes goes badly. But keeping one's composure when disaster strikes is often easier said than done, as a ball out of bounds on one hole may create a mindset of failure, misery, and anger for the next hole. This is due in part to our natural inclination to be somewhat obsessive with outcome and downplaying process – in golf and in life. On the fifth hole, Bud encounters Swami Vivekananda, a twentieth-century Hindu spiritual leader who attempted to demonstrate the linkages between Indian spirituality and Western materialism and "progress." They discuss the virtues of duty and non-attachment.

The Fifth Hole
Vivekananda and Karma-Yoga

Attachment leads to misplaced desire, and misplaced desire leads to suffering. Work can be seen as more than what it is – we need to demand more from it. Leaders need to understand this and to begin to fulfill their primary obligation.

– – – – –

The fifth hole is a 568-yard par five with a rather generous landing area two to three hundred yards off the tee. There is a bit of "death" by several pot bunkers on the right side and if you find yourself in one, there is no clear shot but sideways or backwards out to the fairway. A good long drive makes it possible to be on in two – though once you land on the green, you may have up to a ninety-yard putt to the pin.

The Swami was waiting patiently on the tee for Bud when he arrived with visions of a forthcoming birdie in his mind. Pleasantries over, the men prepared to tee off. Bud, despite being anxious to attack this par five and his run for birdie, offered his new partner the first hit. The Swami genially accepted and slowly and methodically selected his driver, cleaned his ball, tested the wind, and performed two graceful practice swings before teeing his ball up and hitting down the left side of the fairway, carefully avoiding the pot bunkers to the right. Bud teed his ball and nearly jumped out of his shoes in an effort to get close enough for a second shot to the green. Unfortunately, his desire, or rather his passion for distance and his hope for a birdie, overshadowed his normally precise Hogan-like swing. The outcome was a rather direct landing in the deepest pot bunker on the course - pain was his reward. Hmmmm, so much for Nietzsche! Bud was fuming. Par would be a blessing from this position. He turned to the Swami and without a word, appealed to him for guidance.

Swami. Have you ever been to California, Bud?

Bud. Yes, Swami, I have been there many times. Why do you ask?

Swami. Well, I was there many, many years ago - in 1900 to be exact - and gave a speech to a number of academics in Los Angeles. They were all very kind and interested in what this strange man from India had to say about Hinduism and what relevance it could have for the modern world. This is what I told them. "One of the greatest lessons I have learnt in my life is to pay as much attention to the means of work as to its end" (Vivikananda 1999, 5).

Bud. That seems like very good advice, though do you think one might lose sight of the outcome as a result of focussing on process and not product?

Swami. That has not been my experience because the outcome will always arrive - it is a matter of cause and effect, isn't it? If I focus on effect, then I cannot control it. Only by paying attention to the cause can I influence the outcome. So, for example, if I focus all of my attention on the desire to score a four on this par five, then the chances are slim indeed that I will achieve this, as I have forgotten about the pace of my swing, about the landing area for my first and second shot, about the wind, and so on. Without paying heed to these important components of the process of playing this hole, I will undoubtedly fail. On the other hand, if I forget about the score until after I am walking off the green, and if I place all my efforts toward swinging the club smoothly and making smart club selections, then the birdie may arrive without me worrying about it.

Bud. What if I follow your advice and the birdie still does not arrive?

Swami. I am so glad you asked that question, venerable Bud. The answer is … it doesn't matter if it arrives or not.

With that, Bud smiled politely and began to walk toward the pit of hell that had captured his ball. He was wondering who this mystical man was and what in the world he was talking about. He'd thought that the game couldn't get more bizarre after the hole with Nietzsche – but it just had. He stepped down the ladder into the bunker to survey his options. To hit toward the green was impossible; to hit horizontally was possible but a low percentage shot. What made sense was to hit back toward the tee in order to get a decent lie on the fairway. A birdie was out of the question now – he was still thinking of outcome.

Bud selected a wedge and used a quarter swing out of the bunker and then a three wood just short of the green. The Swami hit a one iron and landed the ball on the front fringe. They met again as they strolled toward the green.

Swami. A difficult hole, Bud.

Bud. Yes, and even more so because of my own loss of focus.

Swami. What should your focus be?

Bud. Well, I was just now thinking about what Professor Heidegger said on the third hole about not losing sight of the big picture. And if I combine that with your comment about the means and not the ends, then clearly, to jump ahead in my mind to sinking the birdie putt before I've even hit off the tee is ridiculous if the ultimate goal is a good score at the end of the round. But I need to ask you to clarify what you just said about it not mattering if the birdie comes or not – surely it must matter if the goal is to shoot a low score.

Swami. Precisely, if in fact that is the ultimate goal. But if it isn't the final goal of this complex and silly game, then what is the paramount aim of our involvement? Or as our Greek friend, Aristotle, would ask, "What is the real good that is at stake in golf?" Let me try to explain. We Hindus have a wonderful book called the *Bhagavad-Gita*, which literally means "the song of the lord." In it, we learn about a number of important ideas, not the least of which are non-attachment and something called Karma-Yoga. While the ideas in the *Gita* are definitely connected to Hindu views of deeper metaphysical existence, which need not concern us here, they can also be applied by non-Hindus, as I tried to point out early in the last century to my audience in California.

Let's consider the notion of non-attachment. Here we argue that in order not to experience the disappointment of ends not met or the temporary euphoria of *apparent* goals reached and prizes won, we disregard the outcome (or the *real* good) and focus on what is within our power to control – the means or the process of our actions. To win or lose a battle in a war is of no concern; fighting with honour and dignity to the best of one's ability is the focus. So we remove or detach ourselves from these positive or negative outcomes. If we win, we accept this graciously, nobly; if we lose, we are equally gracious and noble - even if we lose our lives.

Bud. So you are suggesting that I should care little or not at all for the score on a particular hole or on a particular round, as long as I play to the best of my ability and follow the rules of the game. But isn't that a sort of attachment ... to the process? And doesn't this lead to being an unemotional robot? Or to an attitude of "I don't give a damn about anything"? And why then would I play the game at all?

Swami. Ah, excellent points. Consider your attachment to your family. How silly it would be to purposefully live in a detached manner with your wife or your children - taken to an extreme, this would defy the very human attributes of compassion, empathy, even love. However, what the *Gita* is saying is that our strength to detach must be as great as our strength to attach to important things. We must be able to engage with the important people and projects around us with as much strength as we have to disengage from them.

For argument's sake, suppose a man's wife dies before him and he cannot detach himself from the heartache he experiences. If this occurs, he will never again be able to live a fulfilled life. If, on the other hand, after grieving for his wife, he is able to detach and begin anew, then he can live a normal life, benefitting himself as well as his children, friends, and work. Thus we must possess the strength of attachment to certain things with the understanding that we must also have the strength to detach when necessary. Let's get back to golf. We must be able to detach ourselves not only from the bad shot or the bad round, but also from the game of golf altogether, if need be.

Bud. Do you mean walk off the course if a round is going badly?

Swami. No. This would be a reflection of being so attached to outcome that you refuse to engage in the sport and this is not a noble act. It means that at anytime, you have the strength to leave your bag in the basement and never return to it - you have the strength to overcome your desire, which is the cause of your suffering.

Let's take this a step further and discuss Karma-Yoga. Karma, as you probably know, is the belief that good action is rewarded in this or the next life and bad action is punished in this or the next life. This system is the basis of Hindu and Buddhist ethical action, not unlike the more pessimistic "eye for an eye" *quid pro quo* exchange. Yoga refers to spiritual practice, but one based on action rather than meditation. Thus, Karma-Yoga refers to the idea that you can perform your spiritual duty through action. This action is usually associated with work, though it could be extended to everything we do, including golf. What if Jack Nicholas had adopted this perspective? He would have played golf not for hope of winning and receiving money, but rather as a form of duty or prayer detached from outcome - Karma-Yoga. Moreover, if Jack was truly detached, he could have stopped playing golf altogether.

Bud. Well, okay, are you suggesting that I could be doing Karma-Yoga myself as I play?

Swami. Yes.

Bud. And that the score doesn't matter but revealing my noble character, whether I play well or badly, to Krishna, Buddha, God, or myself is the ultimate aim of golf – or anything I do, for that matter?

Swami. Yes.

Bud. All right then, let's talk about work and leadership. The philosophy of work fascinates me, in part because no one really knows how to discuss it or what to discuss – it seems like an unspoken burden that we all must bear.

Swami. I agree with you, Bud. The problem of work as I see it is that we have become too attached to the status of work and much too attached to its financial outcome. The ultimate point of work is not money or production, though these things are not necessarily bad. The ultimate rationale for work is Karma-Yoga, which again means to work nobly, to the best of one's ability, as an offering to humanity and a form of spiritual practice[5] – an offering to one's own self-awareness. Who, I ask you, is the nobler person: the greens keeper who makes every effort to cut the grass as close to the golfers' specifications as possible or the pompous golf instructor who can't teach? Who is the nobler person: the CEO who neglects his family or the caretaker who works two jobs to ensure that her children can pay tuition?

If we perceived work through these lenses, then, frankly, it wouldn't matter what we did, as long as we cared for how we accomplished our duty. Noble work would be measured in terms of our commitment to the process and not to the outcome of our efforts. Now

[5]Spirituality need not be connected with a religious practice but rather with a transrational aspect of the human – that is what goes beyond reason such as meditative thinking.

having said this, the products of our labour will occur and will likely be superior because we have focussed on the means and not the ends, in the same way that our handicap will drop when we stop obsessing about every bad shot we may make.

Mentally exhausted from the long chat down this par five, Bud reached his ball, which was twenty yards short of the green and an unbelievable sixty yards short of the pin. He assessed the situation and thought a bump and run chip with a 6 iron would do the trick. Swami Vivekananda had a forty-yard putt ahead of him and chose to putt with his 1 iron. Bud hit first and ended up with a six-foot putt for par, which he missed. The Swami hit his 1 iron and smacked the pin, leaving a tap-in for birdie. Bud finished the hole and for the first time in years was nonplussed to finish a relatively easy par five with a bogey.

Relevance of Vivekananda

"Process over product" is the essence of the Swami's message, and it may well lead to a sense of calm among those who lead and follow.

His perspective is based on Hindu philosophy in general and on the classic *Bhagavad-Gita* in particular. This famous text is about a prince, Arjuna, who finds himself in personal conflict on the battlefield. Is he to lead his troops into battle and death? Or should he resist the contest, since in this case, the opposition is his kinsmen. As he ponders this dilemma in the middle of the battlefield, he is visited by the Hindu god Vishnu in his avatar form, Krishna. For the remainder of the *Gita*, Krishna explains to Arjuna how his concern for outcome is misguided and beyond his control and comprehension (that is, it is in the hands of Vishnu). Rather than worry about outcome, Krishna counsels him, focus on process and simply let the consequences fall where they may. This is not to suggest that he should be completely fatalistic or complacent. Rather, he must do his duty, which as a prince and warrior is to fight for the right cause despite the fact that the outcome may be out of his control. Further, his performance, and that of any Hindu, is ultimately a form of prayer and respect for Vishnu.

It would be a mistake to ignore this story and its moral simply because one is not a practicing Hindu. As with all philosophies, it is wise to assess what fits, what makes sense in one's own context - to fill the tool box with many instruments. What we can extract from the *Gita* is this - focus on appropriate process and likely the intended outcome will occur. Even if the preferred outcome does not happen, the essential virtue is doing one's best. Experts in sport have advocated this mindset in efforts to overcome competition anxiety and loss of focus due to the overwhelming desire to win. If one follows the game plan and executes one's skills to one's highest capacity, then this in itself is praiseworthy - a win or loss is incidental.

In a leadership context, the *Gita* is essential for those who wish to provide quality service and product. When sales or profits become primary, quality suffers and profits eventually fall. If a salesperson acts morally and is trusted by clients, repeat business occurs and profits expand but only as a secondary outcome of one's noble efforts.

The Driving Range: Putting Theory into Practice

The Swami's main point is this: avoid the trap, and the anxiety that goes along with the trap, of focussing our efforts exclusively on outcome. It requires a leap of faith to believe that our focus on the means will eventually result in the desired outcome and that if these outcomes are not realised, perhaps they were not realistic objectives in the first place based on the resources at hand. So he is telling us to come to terms with the nature of the universe - cause and effect - and to apply this logic to our leadership and work.

The Next Tee...

Golf is a marketer's dream. Why? Because we continue to believe that out there somewhere is the perfect driver that will finally allow us to hit the ball long and straight; out there somewhere is a putter that has been created with all of our foibles in mind, one that will not allow us to miss four-foot putts. We are constantly in search of a reason why we are not responsible for our ball going out of bounds or for our three-putt greens. If we do manage to hit the Olympian long drive or to have a string of good putting, we convince ourselves that it is the new driver or putter, and we guard these clubs with our lives because without them we are returned to being mere mortals. In other words, we fail to take responsibility for our behaviour. But it's not the clubs – it's the player holding onto them that is the problem and the solution. The sixth hole has Bud playing with Jean-Paul Sartre, a philosopher known for his thoughts on freedom, responsibility, and authentic living.

The Sixth Hole
Sartre and Good and Bad Faith

We're in flight from responsibility. Leaders, like good parents, need to create an environment in which free will is acknowledged and responsibility for all behaviour is recognized. A policy has never made a decision – that is a human endeavour.

– – – – –

The sixth hole is a 374-yard par four. Going long off the tee is a bit tricky, as there are two rather nasty bunkers out around the 250-yard mark. The shot to the green is also a challenge, as it sits on a plateau that raises the green about five feet above the fairway. Once there, it's a relatively straightforward putt.

Jean-Paul Sartre sat on the bench beside the sixth tee with his feet barely touching the ground. His black beret was tilted elegantly to the left and his Gitane smouldered in its holder. He stood up as Bud marched toward him in his typical military fashion – "the Colonel's walk," as his kids teasingly called it. They shook hands and Bud was a bit taken aback by the small physical stature of this man – he was 5 feet tall - despite being a giant in the world of philosophy.

Sartre. Monsieur Bud, it is indeed a pleasure to meet you. I understand that you were flying Spitfires over France while I was in the French underground. Luckily, your cannon fire and I never met personally.

Bud. Yes, it was a difficult time and we are blessed to have survived it.

Sartre. Or rather, good decisions resulted in us surviving, wouldn't you say?

Bud had made good decisions all his life, but he still thought that someone had intervened on more than one occasion to save him from an earlier tee-off time in heaven. Sartre placed his Gitane down beside his ball, and with a compact Trevino-like swing, punched his ball barely onto the landing area about 215 yards out. Bud, keeping in mind his conversation with Vivekananda, played a careful 3 wood down the left side, avoiding the two bunkers affectionately known as the "coffins."

Bud. What did you do after the war, Monsieur Sartre?

Sartre. I wrote, mostly, I suppose, and taught as well. The war affected all of us in different ways. For me, it led deeply into philosophy; my therapy, I suppose you could say, was to write. But I didn't just write those weighty books that make students cringe. I also gave many public lectures and wrote plays that I hoped would communicate broadly the message I felt was so important.

Bud. What was the message?

Sartre. To accept that you are free to choose and that you must be responsible for your behaviour.

Bud. Well, that is sound advice, but isn't it common sense?

Sartre. It is anything but common, Monsieur Bud. Inasmuch as we are in flight from deep thinking, as my colleague, Professor Heidegger, suggested to you on the third hole, we are also in flight from taking responsibility for our actions and for honestly acknowledging our own freedom in both our failures and our successes.

We find ourselves in this situation for a number of reasons. First, in many respects, we are - and have always been - hard-wired, as they say, to look to external sources for our misery and happiness. In Homeric times, humans looked to the gods for justification for death and destruction as well as for bounty: "It was Zeus who brought us the plague of flies for our misdeeds."[6] Today we still invoke the will of a supreme being to justify the good and evil that occurs in our world rather than look more deeply at our own moral, economic, and political motivation, insecurity, and responsibility. If it's not a supreme being, then something else becomes the source of our fate - family, friends, organisations, or society at large. Simply put, we believe that we have become who we are because of someone else's doing - not our own. It's a cowardly life we lead.

Bud. So I am a thief because of my environment and not because I have chosen to steal?

Sartre. Oui, c'est vrai!

Sartre reached his ball first and had at least a two hundred-yard shot left to make the green in two. He reached into his bag for a two and a half wood and, with a quick swing, drove his ball to the edge of the plateau, or as the locals called it, "the rampart," which protected the green from the onslaught of golfers. Bud had about 154 yards to the pin and selected an 8 iron. The ball sailed well up into the clouds and *dropped dead* ... four feet from the pin. He didn't see the ball land and strangely he didn't care because he felt he had swung through the ball so well. Perhaps the Swami's wisdom was rubbing off a little.

---

[6]Sartre wrote a play entitled The Flies, in which Zeus brings down a plague of flies on the people of Argos for Agamemnon's murder.

Bud. Back to being a thief. You're right, we all tend to deflect responsibility for our behaviour – from our kids saying that the dog ate their homework to the manager who says her hands are tied because of organisational policy.

Sartre. Yes, it's true, we have a multitude of scapegoats at our disposal for our individual fates and, while religion and society and culture are distant excuses, a more readily available apology for our behaviour is the so-called policy goat.

We in the twentieth, and now into the twenty-first, century have become organisational beings – from the cradle to the grave. As children, we are modelled to become bureaucrats in school as well as in activities such as sports and music. We march to class in lines, sit in neat rows, and regurgitate information back to the teacher in order to achieve acceptable grades that allow us to move up to the next layer of the educational bureaucracy. This continues through secondary school and, for some, through college or university, despite its illusion of free thinking. Once we pass through these gauntlets, we enter into the world of work bureaucracy, where we fulfill roles that someone else has designed and obey orders and accept supervision in exchange for money and security – certainly not for creativity or meaningful work. Since we rarely see the final outcome of anything we do, we feel no responsibility for good or evil that emerges from the organisation, which has, for all intents and purposes, become our parent or our priest. Any decision we make is based upon a policy or a financial statement, and it never seems to be an individual actually making a decision but a rule being implemented. So what has occurred, Monsieur Bud, is that all along the way, we have been trained not to think or choose for ourselves but to rely on the guidance of the architect of the bureaucracy for our behaviour. We are agents of the organisation.

Bud. This seems to be the rationale that Adolph Eichmann used at Nuremburg. Is it not?

Sartre. Oui, Bud, this is what he said, essentially that he was following orders and being a dutiful – that is, an efficient and effective – soldier to the Führer. American soldiers at Abu Ghraib in 2004 argued the same – just following orders. Presumably the shear horror of ISIS is also justified by a false sense of duty to a higher power. The principle behind these kinds of bureaucratic apologies, and pathologies, is subtle yet widespread in the organisational world, and this dissipation of responsibility often results in systemic evil. Now, while evil of this magnitude is rare, what *is* ever present in the organisational world is the loss of both individual responsibility and the acknowledgement of individual responsibility. So the lowly bureaucrat may not commit a crime, he or she may not even hurt another person, but what this individual does contribute to is the organisationally sanctioned kidnapping of the authentic self and its replacement with the inauthentic, valueless, faceless, emotionless worker.

Bud. This sounds like evil on a micro-scale to me, although this has occurred through our efforts to avoid chaos, hasn't it? Also, is it not a response to our efforts to provide and predict the greatest goodness in terms of the most efficient, effective, and productive services, products, and government to the greatest number of people? These intentions are good – though it seems clear that the outcome to the individual is more devastating than most of us would think.

Sartre. Tell me, Bud, how many retired people do you know who would honestly say that they had a fulfilling career? How many people found their work truly meaningful?

Bud. Very few. There are some, but very, very few of those who worked in bureaucracies: only those with power seem to have enjoyed their careers – the rest lived for weekends and retirement. So what's the solution? It's unrealistic to dissolve bureaucracies inasmuch as it's unreal to stop valuing efficiency.

Sartre. This is true. The concept of bureaucracy is not the problem, nor is the problem a concern for getting the task done in a competent manner. The problem is that the individual has been sacrificed, and sacrificed unnecessarily. This is so because of the way in which we have wrongly perceived what drives the human to act.

The French philosopher walked up to his ball just below the rampart and gently, with a sand wedge, floated his ball up toward the pin. It landed and skipped backward about five feet. Bud carefully surveyed the line to the cup and then confidently stroked in his first birdie. He looked up just in time to see a small café (*Cafe de Flore*) appear behind the green. He watched as Sartre walked past his ball toward a beautiful woman waiting for him – the smell of Gitane and espresso wafted in the air, along with the sound of Miles Davis playing "Blue." Bud smiled to himself and strolled on to the seventh tee, where he saw two men arguing.

Relevance of Sartre

Freedom and responsibility … are they antithetical to leadership? Sartre was not the first to discuss these concepts, but he was one of the more forceful in convincing us that we need to break free from culture, society, and religion in order to choose for ourselves what we want to become. He argues that fundamentally we are beings with the capacity to choose freely. What's more, we have an obligation to take responsibility for this freedom and we must not lay blame elsewhere. Society and religion have for too long provided us with excuses for not exercising our freedom and for not taking responsibility for what we do.

Society, culture, religion, and, to a significant extent, science have led us to believe that much of who we are and will be is predestined. Sartre disagrees with this perspective. We may well be born with brown hair and green eyes, but we were not born to be accountants or wheat farmers – these are choices we make ourselves or decisions made by others to whom we have succumbed. Sartre argues that our task in life is to make ourselves aware of the traps of inauthenticity that are all around us (God's will or the DSM-V) and to strive to make decisions that are true for us. This does not mean that we will become anarchists unable to function in society or in organisations. It means that when we choose, our choices are based on information and we know what the implications may be for us and others. We do not act because someone has told us to do so; we act because we have thought about it and understand what we are getting into, whether it is marriage or joining a new company. This existential perspective, as you can imagine, played out well in the bohemian world of the Parisian Cafe de Flore, but in the corporate context, acknowledging and (heaven forbid) fostering freedom is at odds with the neo-Tayloristic mindset of many leaders.[7] Best to maintain control over workers to ensure

[7] F.W. Taylor was an early twentieth-century theorist who promoted the notion of time and motion studies to make work (particularly in factories) more efficient and effective. The criticism was that while the accuracy of physical movements improved, the participation of the worker-as-craftsman was forever lost.

quality service and product: they are not here to be enlightened – they are here to earn a wage.

Taylorism and its many incarnations and affiliations (behaviourism, for example) works – in the short term. Bureaucracies are established, rules are created, boundaries are set and work life is stifled – but the job gets done despite the fact that we are miserable doing it. We live for pay, security, and weekends. Underlying all of this is (1) a basic mistrust of workers (left to their own devices, they will not perform) and (2) the perception that workers need us to tell them what to do.

A Sartrean leader sees all of this differently. While the organisational goals must be reached, they need not be reached with workers-as-automatons. Individual workers bring the potential to be creative and to find their work meaningful. The leader's job, then, is to create an environment in which individuals have reasonable access to their creative will and can be held responsible for their successes and failures. This leader would seek to understand his or her employee as a person with an inner need to flourish at work – as opposed to simply a role-filler. While productivity would, of course, be necessary, it would emerge from an environment where individuals would be authentically engaged in their work, regardless of what it is. This is the mark of the transformational leader, one who knows, engages, listens, and appreciates employees. This moves beyond the transactional leader, who merely follows the rules and fails to interpret them within a context and understanding that is meaningful for the individual and the organisation as a whole.

The Driving Range: Putting Theory into Practice

Sartre, like all existential philosophers, believes that free will is the starting point for all human activity. To avoid it, forget about it, or deny its existence is to live inauthentically. And if the purpose of human life is to seek authenticity, then we need to accept our freedom, however difficult and painful it may be at times, and to take responsibility for this freedom in all of our behaviour. Praise and blame are always ours to bear. This has a profound impact on the manner in which we as leaders perceive our job and on the expectations of those who choose to follow us. We accept that we are free to choose all our actions, we expect the same of our employees, we accept responsibility for failure and success – and this goes for employees as well.

The Next Tee...

Why do we play golf? For pleasure? Or to overcome ourselves and our environment? Playing for pleasure is instinctual – we are happy when we play well and unhappy when we play badly. This feeling of happiness or frustration may affect us subconsciously for a day or a week until the next time we get a chance to play. Our partners certainly experience this euphoria or dejection when we return home from our five hours of recreation. Playing for conquest is more intentional. We review the weather and the clothes we will wear, we prepare our clubs (all of which are based on the most innovative technology), and we strategize our game plan using the latest golf theory at our disposal. Our goal is to play better than we did the last round, to beat our opponent (despite the fact that it is a "friendly" game), and to show the golf course who is boss. Success confirms our line of attack; failure results in a sense of personal inadequacy and a return to the drawing board to evaluate the strengths and weaknesses of our plan in order to overcome our faults the next time out. Pleasure and power seem to be the basis for why we play this game and for our behaviour in the workplace as well. On the seventh hole, Bud encounters two philosopher-psychologists who try to convince him of the virtues of their theories of motivation.

The Seventh Hole
Freud and Adler – Pleasure and Power

It is presumed to be a given that pleasure and/or power are what make us tick in life. We are controlled by the need to satisfy these drives and to overcome what we lack. The organisation thrives on this knowledge.

– – – – –

The seventh hole is a 388-yard par four. There is no forgiveness between the tee and the start of the fairway. The first stroke needs to be straight and reasonably long to avoid the thick gorse that separates the tee from the landing area. From there, it is a relatively straightforward approach to the green, but there will be trouble if you're short because of two large bunkers and trouble if you're too long because of the potential for a lengthy putt.

The two men on the tee were involved in a heated discussion when Bud cautiously approached. Upon his arrival, the two broke up their debate and instantly changed their demeanour to that of gracious hosts welcoming Bud. With very heavy German accents, they welcomed him to the seventh hole. A short exchange of pleasantries took place while each checked scorecards for yardage and what club to use.

Freud. Herr Graland, we have been expecting you. I see you have survived the ordeal of playing with that insufferable Monsieur Sartre. Imagine believing that our behaviour is based upon free will! He's the typical philosopher - all talk and no empirical proof.

Adler. Interesting, I don't recall you measuring an ego, Dr. Freud. Now, Herr Bud, tell us what club you prefer for this unspeakable hole. I'm going to use a 1 iron and throw caution to the wind.

A bold move, thought Bud. Boldness is definitely a necessary ingredient for successful moral leadership but it can be used in a misguided fashion for immoral objectives. He was wondering how best to approach this with Adler when he had finished his stroke, but when the good doctor over swung and his ball went into deep trouble, Bud thought he'd better wait. Then Freud, ever imperious, came onto the tee, with a 5 wood. Saying nothing, he quite simply teed his ball and made a perfect swing, and his ball bounced freely on the distant fairway. He then looked to Bud with his customary pleasant facial expression, conveying the obvious: "Beat zat!" And Bud, also with a 5 wood, did just that, surprising himself more than the others. As Adler went his own way to search out his errant ball in futility, Bud and Freud strolled down the fairway.

Bud. Dr. Freud, that shot obviously gave you great pleasure. What pleasure can be found in leadership?

Freud. Oh dear! That's a good one. As you know, I have staked my life's work on the idea that pleasure is the dominant force guiding what we do. There's nothing really magical about this. All we have to do is observe ourselves and others to see that pleasure is really what motivates us. Ultimately, we are pleasure-seeking creatures. And this is especially so in leadership.

Bud. Is pleasure an end unto itself? And everything else a means to that end?

Freud. Absolutely, Herr Bud! Pleasure can only be achieved by doing something. Indeed, even thinking can give us pleasure. But when you mention leadership, then simply thinking is not enough because if all one does is think, then there is no leadership at all. Leaders *do* things and they do them for pleasure, although to the casual observer that might not always seem the case. But there is a tie between what Professor Adler says about power and what I say about pleasure, and that is that power is in itself a pleasure trip, or as some might say, a "turn-on." And you know, we should not be one bit surprised about this because we humans have highly complex biochemical structures. Look at those athletes who seem to endure all sorts of aches and pains yet continue to "go out there and do it." Even jogging is a painful trauma to the body, but forever and a day we see joggers "loving it," and that "loving it" is ultimately chemistry. They get a high from the chemicals that enable the body to endure stress.

Bud. Same goes for leaders?

Freud. Yes, of course! Leadership is all about having visions – doesn't make any difference what kind – and leaders know full well that they need others to make those visions a reality: they can't go it alone. So what leaders do is create those visions in others – I think the common term is *empowerment* – thereby getting them to do the leader's bidding. And then they too get a sense of pleasure in doing this because they have let their minds become instruments of what the leader wants. It's all quite a fascinating undertaking.

Bud. But there has to be more to leadership than simply acting out the pleasure principle. We all know that leadership can be downright painful, both physical and psychological.

Freud. But of course! All means to ends are not smooth sailing – or flying. Bumpy weather is the constant companion of any pilot. You know that. Same goes for leadership. No pain, no gain – is that not what we hear in all our training programs? This is the exercise of my reality principle, which means that the immediate world confronting us directly causes the ego to proceed with caution regarding the pursuit of pleasure. This helps leaders endure those unpleasant experiences we all face. In my language, it's the ego telling the id, the storehouse of pleasure, not to get too upset: these unpleasant encounters, these stressors, are expected "bumpy means" that will be taken care of. The thing to keep in mind, Bud, is that we humans are driven to further our existence – and the future of our species – through pleasure. And by pleasure I mean a satisfying experience, not merely something that's all bubbly, bouncy, and beautiful. There are dark sides to what we are.

Bud. But how do you account for moral leadership? Is there a moral dimension to the pleasure principle?

Freud. Oh, dear, Herr Bud. Keep in mind that our sole reason for being, our *raison d'être,* is to further our species. And it is our pleasure principle, that which enables us to cope with the stresses we all face that gets us through the day. As we progress – as we evolve as a species, as the great Darwin says – we think about good and evil, right and wrong, in many of our actions. These thoughts are consequences of our evolutionary progress. We invoke such thinking to enhance our well-being. But the crucial point is that these notions of good and evil, right and wrong, are inventions that our minds have created as means to an end, where the means appear troublesome yet the end remains constant: the pleasure of advancing what we are as humans.

Bud. So is moral leadership an invention we have created to get us through the day?

Freud. Absolutely! In a way, moral leadership is an illusion because the moral aspect exists only in our minds. Moral leadership is merely a mechanism employed by leaders to enhance follower support. If followers perceive their leaders to be moral, regardless of how those leaders interpret morality, there is a strong likelihood that followers will do the bidding of their leaders. We all know that most of us have to work for a living - pay bills, put food on the table - and smart leaders know this. So what they do is create work environments that take advantage of the need for followers having to work in the first place. Now, the workers know only too well that they have to work and more often than not, such activity is not really all that pleasurable. So the workers try their best to convince themselves that there is pleasure in the workplace, somewhere. Quite specifically, they create a reality about what they do that enables them to believe they are enjoying, or getting pleasure from, at least some aspects of their work. Consider the caste system in India. How does the individual in a lower caste, such as the Shudra, rationalise his existence in daily 'unskilled toil'? He does it by accepting the belief that this toil will be rewarded by pleasure...eventually in subsequent lives. And leaders tap into this mindset, creating another illusion: "Yes, there is pleasure in what you do." This is cleverly obtained by leaders, creating a culture whereby members do what is perceived to be morally (or religiously) correct. But you will never hear any discussion about just what the word *moral* means. The realities of good and evil that make authentic moral leadership possible are never discussed. That discussion can never take place because it would undermine the illusions created by leaders.

Bud. So leaders create an image of moral leadership that is specifically geared to get followers to buy into what leaders ultimately want: the achievement of their own vision.

Freud. Now you have it.

By this time, Adler had finally managed to get his ball onto the fairway with a *foot mashie*,[8] and he had joined up with Bud and Freud, sensing that a deep conversation was taking place between them. Bud looked somewhat disturbed as if his fundamental beliefs about life had been shaken up. Freud, on the other hand, looked positively delighted and was displaying an unusual grin – the Cheshire cat.

Adler. Now, what have you two been up to? And don't tell me it was all about this wretched game that only proves how hitting a tiny ball with a long stick can drive one insane.

Freud. In need of a little counselling, Herr Professor? Power problems?

Bud could hardly contain his laughter at Freud's needling. He was aware that some discord had developed between Freud and Adler. They were so different, not only in their views of human nature but even more so in their dress, with Freud ever the

[8]Foot mashie is a term used to describe a golfer kicking the ball out of the rough rather than hitting it with a club. It is against the rules!

impeccable – almost dashing – academic, whereas Adler looked like he had slept in his clothes.

Bud's shot to the green was right on the money, leaving about a five-footer for a birdie. Freud's was quite off the mark, ending in a bunker, and Adler's fairway shot was a great recovery from his troubles in the gorse, ending inside Bud's on the green. Bud took the opportunity to get Adler's views on leadership.

Bud. Tell me, Professor Adler, what are your thoughts on leadership?

Adler. Are you planning on being here all day?

Bud. Not really, but leadership *is* a complex phenomenon, isn't it?

Adler. Yes, it is. And for me, the essential element is this: leaders must come to the realisation that what they are all about is the betterment of society – they are not entirely about themselves. You see, the major obstacle facing all leaders is the battle of balancing their own drives for overcoming their inferiority complexes with the drive to make society a better place for all. Not an easy task, as you can imagine.

Bud. Is leadership really all about overcoming inferiority complexes?

Adler. Oh yes, that is a major component. But there is another component that accompanies this unavoidable drive, and that is, in one word, power.

Bud. Dr. Freud sees power as some sort of pleasure trip. Do you buy into that?

Adler. Not really. Dr. Freud's problem is that his obsession with the pleasure principle unfortunately clouds his better judgment as to how we humans go about trying to make society better. I believe that power is the medium through which we as individuals achieve, or attempt to achieve, some degree of control over our separate destinies. You see, it's important to understand that when we come into this world we are saddled with all sorts of feelings of inferiority and insecurity. And in order to overcome these feelings, we develop *fictions* about ideals, ideals that we see as useful for overcoming our inferiorities and insecurities. Think about how often you hear phrases like "the average person" or "the average male" or "the average female," and, to bring our conversation back to leadership, "the average worker." None of these exist in reality. They are composites that we have generated to help us deal with contentious social issues and to advance our individual selves.

Bud. Does the phrase *moral leadership* describe a fiction, as you use that word?

Adler. Ah! Now that's a good one! The problem with moral leadership is the misunderstanding that we have some sort of dual mechanism guiding us when faced with issues we interpret as good, bad, right, wrong - one part of us thinks we have some sort of immaterial substance called "free will," whereas the other part of us, correctly so, acknowledges that we are nothing more than the sum total of our genes. The truth of the matter is that through the forces of evolution, we strive for superiority over what we are, especially so in the matter of our inferiorities. This striving for superiority - or perfection, if you will - is at the heart of our drives: it's what makes us do what we do. There are no fictions with any of this. But as for the belief that we have free will guiding us through the swamps of good, bad, right, wrong – well, that really is a fiction. So yes, moral leadership is a fiction, an ideal we have constructed to help us deal with complex leadership situations.

Bud. Well, what about followers? Are they not also striving for perfection, striving to overcome their inferiorities?

Adler. Of course they are. We all are. Most of us have to work for a living, pay bills, that sort of thing. That's a given of the human condition. And as most of us know, we really don't have many options as to what sort of work we do or where we do it. Nonetheless, we understand that work is part of what we are all about, and that understanding helps to generate a sense of overcoming our inferiorities. We see work as a means through which we can, in fact, become better, as it were. At least, we like to think so. So we convince ourselves that what we do is really necessary, not only for our own benefit but also for the benefit of others.

Bud. Does this mean that as a worker I engage my will to co-operate for the benefit of others as well as myself?

Adler. Yes, you could say that. Keep in mind that our will to power is a force within us that enables us to cope. Some of us are more capable at handling interpersonal situations or have a greater drive to overcome obstacles, and it is these who become leaders. If the drive for power is weak, leadership will most often be only a dream. But for some, the will to power is interpreted as a call within the self to become a leader, regardless of where or what type of organisation.

Bud. Are there fictions here?

Adler. The only fiction in any leadership undertaking is the idea that morals are critical. We exist, as human beings, to improve the quality of life of others and this necessitates leadership. The guiding forces here are consequences of evolutionary forces. Leaders invoke ideas like "moral leadership" to enhance co-operation and support from followers. Astute leaders are aware that we are all engaged in an evolutionary process aimed at making life better all round, to perfect our species. There is nothing magical like the operation of free will to make this happen. Most of us are totally unaware of the nature of these evolutionary forces. We quite simply do not understand what is going on. And yes, this is where fictions play crucial roles: the belief, for example, that we live in a moral universe, if you will; that we can, in fact, make crucial moral-laden decisions. And we do just that, some of us more often than others. But the bottom line is that the decision-making process is inherent in our evolutionary process. In a word, it's chemistry.

As the three tallied their strokes, both Freud and Adler thanked Bud for his thought-provoking questions and suggested that he not waste his time thinking too much about matters that will ultimately be settled by biochemistry. Bud, on the other hand, was not convinced that chemistry holds all the answers. Maybe environments have a lot to do with leadership: no one would argue that, he thought. So who better to have that conversation with on the next hole than B.F. Skinner, Mr. Reinforcement.

Relevance of Freud

Freud's philosophy of what we are as humans and how we get along with others, the active ingredients of social bonding, is rooted in the unconscious. The challenge lies in how to integrate the unconscious with the conscious in leadership activity. What we see from relevant literature is that there really is no research linking the unconscious with the conscious. What is most unfortunate about Freud in the context of leadership is his undying admiration for Charles Darwin, whom he consistently refers to as "the great Darwin." Freud became sidetracked by Darwin's overpowering influence. Darwin placed us on the evolutionary stage along with all other living creatures; the regrettable assumption was/is that humankind thus lost its uniqueness in possessing an internal moral compass, that which has the potential to affect moral order in the universe. This moral capacity, of course, is the ultimate ingredient in all leadership, an ingredient that we all too often see slip by the wayside. We are so accustomed to linking Freud with dreams and troubled souls lying on couches awaiting a white-bearded saviour to cleanse neurotic minds that we lose sight of his impact on leadership. Put quite simply, according to Freud, we are not much different from the animals all around us; humans are not a special species with inborn capabilities for making moral judgments. We do not engage in meaningful dialogue about what makes humans different from other species; in fact, we seldom if ever discuss why we exist at all. These two issues of "what we are" and "why we are" are central to any intelligent and meaningful leadership process, but this kind of discussion is impossible within the context of Freudian thinking.

The tragedy of Freudian thinking for leadership is that from a moral perspective the criterion for moral action is anchored in the group, the culture of the organisation. Every day we see senior leaders of business, government, religions lie, cheat, and steal. This of course creates an atmosphere of fear for those members who might have serious thoughts about doing what they perceive to be proper moral action. We know these individuals as whistleblowers. These individuals more often than not do not survive in the organisation. Because we continue to suffocate ourselves with the morality of the herd, contemporary leaders in all organisations lie, cheat, and steal. This creates a culture of fear for one's job and prevents strategic risk taking; the atmosphere is one of distrust and repression, and the workplace is dominated by transactional behaviours and attitudes: "The boss is always right," "The policies say …" or "That is the way we do things around here." The transformational leader, on the other hand, acts with integrity, enabling and valuing family, employees, and community.

Relevance of Adler

Central to the context of leadership are Adler's notions of perfection and striving, captured in his imperatives, "Achieve! Arise! Conquer!" "The striving for perfection is innate in the sense that it is part of life, a striving, an urge, a something without which life would be unthinkable" (Ansbacher et al. 1956, 104). But we need to be reminded that perfection is a relative term and dependent on many human characteristics, motivations, and rewards, both extrinsic and intrinsic.

Two leadership-related issues from Adler are power and fictions, where the former is a clear given and the latter is virtually unheard of. We all know that most leaders are power-oriented, whether for good or ill. For Adler, power is not a good thing because of its threat to the perfection of social interest - the condition of humanity that can never be achieved but that we inherently strive to achieve. Power is contextual as well; although it surrounds us in our entire daily willing and doing, it is silent until we bump up against a power differential. For example, if the use of power in the workplace is fair, we access its benefits, creative thinking and so on. But if we encounter power as a negative, then it serves to distance employees from their reasons for productivity.

Adler's contribution to the study of leadership is tied to his notions of striving for perfection, social interest, power, and fictions. Collectively, they represent most of Adler's thinking about what we are and why we do what we do: we are driven (strive) to enhance the betterment of society (social interest) through the use of power (evil though it is because it is a threat to social interest) and delusional thinking (fictions). Leaders who follow in these footsteps will most likely be charismatic, creating images of what followers want to hear, and there is no shortage of such leaders and followers. Although knowing this to be a potential issue in leadership can create a sense of suspicion about someone as a leader if their actions betray their words, there will always be those who blindly follow at their own peril.

Adler has much to offer to the study of leadership, especially in his ideas about striving for perfection. If this alone is elaborated upon and emphasized in leadership exercises, seminars, and actual practice, then society will certainly be much better off. But it would be a serious mistake to integrate other dominant aspects of Adler's thinking, especially his ideas about fictions, because they distort what it is to be a human being. His notion of power, which is a key component of his work, is obviously central to all leadership, but its use can be for good or evil, as we all know. The problem is that people who use power for their personal gain do so either because they know of no other way to achieve their own perfection and/or are unaware of others who need to experience perfectionism in their own right. The collective of many people striving for perfection in a positive way creates a whole (an organisation) that is foundationally solid and more resilient to disruptions.

Leaders do not constantly think about power; they do not wake up in the morning and say to themselves, "I shall exercise power today." Power for leaders is like our internal autonomic systems - it's out of the person's conscious control - but for some, this internal autonomic power grid literally drives the self. And it is here where good and evil become outcomes: when leaders fail to consider the moral aspects of what they do, the potential for evil is apparent. The only way to deal with this is to keep in mind Adler's notion of striving for perfection, which translates into helping others maximize, enhance, and "perfect" what exists within others.[9]

The Driving Range: Putting Theory into Practice

Freud's message is simple: enjoy life with all its pleasures; don't get hung up over moral-laden issues and religious influences because both are really nothing more than illusions that we have created to help us make society better. Our existence has one sole purpose and that is to procreate the species. So in business, do what is best for business and don't get caught up in the feelings

[9] See James McGregor Burns (1979) for a more detailed discussion of transformational leadership.

of others: doing so will simply get in the way of what's good for the business. Freud's message comes directly from Charles Darwin: our existence is purely and simply about "survival of the fittest." Adler's message for us is quite different from Freud's in that Adler sees our existence as the means by which we perfect what's within us. For the businessperson, this means doing what is best for the organisation, where the organisation is really a means through which we all become better. The driving mechanism is power: we covet power because power enables us to achieve our particular goals, and ideally, one of those goals ought to be the betterment of humanity.

The Next Tee...

According to Bud's next partner, it is probable that all of our behaviour on and off the golf course has been conditioned by our environment. This is particularly true in the realm of leadership and work, where we are constantly faced with reward and punishment for our good and bad behaviour – free will is a chimera. Clearly that ball you just hit out of bounds was not your fault – it was just the result of a bad learning environment. Blame your teaching pro and get your money back!!

The Eighth Hole
B.F. Skinner and Conditioning a Good Swing

Free will is either wishful thinking or a potential curse on the organisation. Organisations depend on human programming – otherwise why would we accept meaningless toil as the dominant feature of our lives?

– – – – –

The eighth hole is the only par three on the front nine. It is a tricky 175 yards to the pin due to the fact that the green is hidden from the tee area and guarded by two bunkers. In addition, this green is extremely large and is shared with the tenth hole.

Bud was quite aware of the influence of B.F. Skinner's work on reinforcement and conditioning, not only on the American psyche but also on the world at large. Bud had read his famous - or infamous - *Walden Two*, Skinner's quest for Utopia. Whatever one might think of him and his psychology, Bud was not prepared to dismiss him outright for the simple reason that his ideas about reinforcement made a lot of sense. Bud was also ready to acknowledge that Skinner could help him out with his golf swing. As for leadership - well, he wanted to hear from the man himself on that one.

Bud. Hello, Dr. Skinner. It's very nice to meet you. How are you doing?

Skinner. Don't ask. I just double-bogeyed the last three holes and am looking for someone to blame. It appears that my golfing environment has been corrupted. But never mind that. How are you doing?

Bud. Very well, considering who I have been playing with for the past seven holes. This entire round has been, without question, the most surreal I have ever experienced. I'm feeling a bit disembodied actually. Do you think good golf is mind over matter?

Skinner. I suppose you could say that, although I never was a big fan of mind. I never did figure out what it was. Waste of time.

Bud. But wouldn't you agree that the trouble with a lot of golfers, and perhaps leaders too, is that they psych themselves out - or into - trouble?

Skinner. True enough, but that can be overcome through my conditioning procedures.

Bud. Is there a difference between conditioning the body and conditioning the mind?

Skinner. For me, the mind is a machine, a machine made up of fibres that carry electrical impulses. We can control the flow of that electrical energy by focussing on what we want to control. For example, let's see your golf swing. Take a mulligan - no one's watching.

Bud. Sounds like a good idea.

Bud bent down to grab a few blades of grass and tossed them into the air to test the wind. All was calm - an easy 7 iron was the choice to make. He fashioned a smooth three-quarter swing and sailed the ball to the back of the green - a long putt for birdie coming up. Dr. Skinner, whose slight physique was the direct result of his lack of sleep (allegedly three hours a night) and lack of physical *conditioning*, selected a 3 wood. Though he skulled his ball off the tee, it managed to miss the bunkers and roll just short of the green.

Skinner. Ah, Bud, you've played this game before, I can see that. You don't have any swing problems. As a matter of fact, your swing is far better than mine.

Bud. Comes from practice, I guess.

Skinner. Well, of course it does. Everything we do well is an outcome of practice, something that I call "habit." And the more we strengthen that habit, the better the behaviour, whatever that may be.

Bud. Would you say that all types of behaviour can be improved through habit? Or is habit not appropriate for some behaviours?

Skinner. Not sure what you have in mind there, Bud. There I go again, using that word "mind" when I really don't know what it is. Anyway. What's on your mind?

Bud. Well, I was thinking of something like leadership, for example. I can't see how conditioning works in that realm because leadership exercises are just the opposite of golf swings: no two leadership exercises are the same, whereas with the golf swing, that behaviour is forever habituated, with only minor adjustments here and there.

Skinner. Yes and no. Leadership, as I see it, is an exercise where someone, the leader, gets others, the followers, to do his or her bidding. This is really learned behaviour using strategies for such things as reading the followers and choosing certain techniques to motivate them. That's what leadership is all about, as far as I can tell. Wouldn't you agree to that?

Bud. You make it sound so simple, Dr. Skinner. And in a way, you're right. But how about leadership that involves moral-laden issues? In that type of situation, a leader is really a teacher, teaching the followers about the nuances and complexities of the moral dimension involved. You can't really condition someone to do the right thing, the good thing, as is the case with a golf swing.

Skinner. Your problem, Bud, is that you're too much the philosopher and not enough the psychologist.

Bud. What does that mean?

Skinner. Philosophers play mind games. They play with myths as if they're the real thing – like that golf ball. There's no science to philosophers whatsoever, so they really don't help anyone in any way. Instead, they confuse everyone. Psychologists, on the other hand, are trained to analyze human behaviour using the scientific method. This is precisely what professional golfers do: they observe the golf swing very carefully, analytically, and make whatever adjustments are necessary. Same goes for leadership. Or at least it should. And most of the psychological approaches are, in fact, science based. Leadership runs into problems when philosophers start meddling in areas of human behaviour that really require the expertise of scientifically trained psychologists.

Bud. Can science really help leaders facing moral situations?

Skinner. Absolutely! No question about it. All these issues of right and wrong, good and bad, are really nothing more than consequences of our environmental influences through conditioning. There is no inherent good, bad, right, or wrong. When we refer to actions in those terms, we are actually talking about behaviours that are brought about by various reinforcement strategies. Quite simple, really.

Bud. But what about free will? And ethical decision making? We can't condition our free will, can we?

Skinner. There you go again, Bud, being the philosopher. That'll get you in trouble every time. Free will is a myth created by humans to help explain how they cope, how they make decisions.

Bud. But we are held responsible for what we do. This is what goes on in the courts, from everyday minor offences to international issues such as crimes against humanity. How does conditioning fit in with those scenarios?

Skinner. Being responsible is nothing more than learned or unlearned behaviour. If you fail to learn, then you pay a penalty. That's what conditioning is all about.

Bud. But I like to think that I have some sort of control over what I do, especially in a leadership situation. What you're saying is that my line of thinking on this is just an illusion. That everything I do, even actions with moral implications, is nothing more than conditioned responses. Is that what you're saying to me?

Skinner. You got it right, Bud. Now, let's get on with this game, even though some refer to it as 'a good walk spoiled'.

Bud. Dr. Skinner, tell me about organisations and learned behaviour.

Skinner. They are fascinating examples of group conditioning, aren't they? It never ceases to amaze me how so many "individuals" can be controlled by so few. And it gives credence to the behavioural fact that so many "good and intelligent people" can do such evil. If there were such a thing as innate conscience, as opposed to conditioned response, would we have any of the misery caused by systemic evil in this world? I think not. Control the environment and you control and predict behaviour. Just review for a moment the more popular leadership and motivational theories. They are intentionally or unintentionally based in behavioural psychology. If I want an employee to do X, I find out what motivates the individual. Here's where Freud and Adler are partially correct: some are motivated by pleasure, usually in the form of money or security; others respond to opportunities for status and power – titles or corner offices, for example. Some theories are more sophisticated than this, since they try to link personal values with corporate values to create a seamless bond between what is good for the individual and what is good for the organisation. And reciprocally, what is bad for the organisation must then also be bad for the individual as an agent of the institution. The infamous Nazi Adolf Eichmann is a case in point.

Bud. Okay, I agree that humans can be rather sheep-like, but is it a function of conditioning or a lack of awareness of free will?

Skinner. Bud, there you go again – free will is a pipe dream. On this point, my colleagues Freud and Adler agree with me. There is no such thing as free will: we are animals. Any leader must be thrilled by this because it means that with proper training and reinforcement, the vast majority of employees will indeed follow because they have no choice if conditioning is done well. So we can control these human sheep to do profound good, and if exposed to an evil leader with enough power, the sheep can also be used as tools of wickedness.

Bud. So Eichmann was as blameless as the kid who steals a car or the executive who pads a budget?

Skinner. Correct. They are all products of their environment.

Dr. Skinner chipped his ball to within four feet of the cup, a performance due to hours on the practice green – conditioning. He stroked the ball three feet past and then missed the par putt – a dry patch on the green. Free will an illusion? A logical argument, perhaps, thought Bud, but one that is based upon a premise that may be difficult to prove. What if he's wrong?

Relevance of Skinner

Of all that Skinner has written and that others have written about him, only two sources pertain directly to leadership: *Walden Two* (1948) and *Beyond Freedom and Dignity* (1972). Without doubt, Skinner has had a positive influence upon leadership thinking and practice, especially through his concept of reinforcement, a staple of all social interaction. What ought to be of concern for students of leadership are Skinner's ideas about what we are as human beings. *Walden Two* is his modern-day utopic novel based on the "science" of human behaviour known as reinforcement. The overarching problem here is what we know as free will, which Skinner dismisses as a non-issue buried in the ongoing free will-versus-predestination debate. In discussing this with fellow observers of his utopia, Skinner says,

> Doesn't he know he's merely raising the old question of predestination and free will? All that happens is contained in an original plan, yet at every stage the individual seems to be making choices and determining the outcome. The same is true of Walden Two. Our members are practically always doing what they want to do – what they "choose" to do – but we see to it that they will want to do precisely the things which are best for themselves and the community. Their behaviour is determined, yet they're free. (Skinner 1948, 296)

To reinforce his views on this in a global perspective, he writes: "We mean to ask what a few men can make of mankind. And that's the all-absorbing question of the twentieth century. What kind of world can we build – those of us who understand the science of behaviour?" (Skinner 1948, 297).

Let's assume for a moment that notions of good and evil are part and parcel of all leadership activity – a fair assumption to make. Next, consider this from *Walden Two*: "Our conception of man is not taken from theology but from a scientific examination of man himself. And we recognize no revealed truths about good or evil or the laws or codes of a successful society" (199). The first part of this statement is non-problematic: the application of science to aid us in understanding what we are is categorically essential. And progress is clearly being made here, especially in the chemical analysis of the brain. But when such an approach is linked to the second part of the statement, then humanity has lost its pivotal point of demarcation from lower organisms: what is good and evil is a consequence of conditioning techniques by others, not by our individual selves. The entire notion of individual responsibility is gone, and all that is evil is merely a consequence of inappropriate or dysfunctional conditioning.

Beyond Freedom and Dignity is Skinner's more direct statement about the issues raised in *Walden Two* twenty-four years earlier. His central tenet is that we are mere animals with no special equipment to make informed decisions about what is good and what is evil. All such prescriptions and proscriptions are, in reality, consequences of conditioning by our interactions with our external environment. Nothing exceeds the following in this regard:

> The behaviours classified as good or bad and right or wrong are not due to goodness or badness, or a good or bad character, or a knowledge of right and wrong; they are due to contingencies involving a great variety of reinforcers, including the general verbal reinforcers of "Good!" "Bad!" "Right!" and "Wrong!" (Skinner 1972, 113).

In a sense, much of this is true not only in what is available in print for leadership but certainly in how leadership is actually conducted. These verbal reinforcers are ingrained in all leadership lexicons. But, and this is a big but, is that all there is to leadership? Current literature is about equally pro and con.

Toward the end of *Beyond Freedom and Dignity*, Skinner is ever so forceful in relegating us all to the status of lower organisms. Whether or not leaders are concerned about or even give the slightest nod to the morality of their behaviour, Skinner provides very serious commentary. What leaders and those conducting leadership seminars do about this will impact severely on how humanity progresses.

The bottom line for Skinner in the context of leadership is that we are humanoids, robots with human form, flesh, and bones. This approach to what we are makes for the best of leaders in a world where anything of substance regarding morality of leadership is disguised, masked, and toyed with. In the marketplace, what one can get away with dictates a moral code captured in that perennial children's game: "I'm the king of the castle and you're not." Abundant success goes to those leaders immersed in "me first" thinking, where plotting and gauging success is judged solely in monetary terms. Authentic notions of trusting others, caring for others, or concern for others are signs of weakness. But playing the counterfeit game assures leaders of assuming positions of power and authority, ultimately for their own satisfaction.

The question of leadership always returns to the notion of what is "good leadership." This question has three interconnected perspectives. The first is what we do and why and how we do it, the second is what we do not do and why we do not do it, and the third, which is less obvious, is how I as a leader find others to help when I find my own leadership faltering. Transformational leadership defies the mere application of method. The key to leadership is not found within the method itself - in other words, by following a series of steps toward effective leadership. Rather, effective leadership lies in the act of interpreting the method in personal contexts. The value of seeking a philosophical perspective on leadership is in its long-term application, which is able to guide the leader through both good and challenging times. In this context, leadership is lifted from the books and seminars, and comes to life in the shifting realities of the world. Methods are signposts to keep one alert to the comings and goings within a leadership role, but effective leadership requires that the leader interpret methods into practice through multiple understandings.

The Driving Range: Putting Theory into Practice

Skinner's message is that we are what we are as a consequence of environmental influences. Notions of good, bad, right, and wrong have absolutely nothing to do with internal characteristics or traits of a human being. Rather, such terms are nothing more than the verbal reinforcers we use to get the desired behaviours we want from others – and from ourselves as well. We're all animals: hybrid animals, yes, but animals nonetheless. Don't be fooled by thoughts of moral imperatives or religious dictates because they are all illusions, systems of reinforcement schedules and protocols set up to get the desired behaviours.

The Next Tee...

Golf drives people crazy. We focus on our score, and one bad shot can put the average person into a panic. We all know that. But every now and then we play with someone who, despite playing badly, seems to remain calm, even happy, as if the score didn't matter. Vivekananda spoke of this earlier in the round when he argued that we should focus on process only, with the assumption that outcomes will follow only if the means are respected. Our next player sees golf and work in a similar fashion. They are mediums through which we find meaning, not ends in and of themselves. When they are perceived as ends only, we panic over apparently failed goals. But if we see golf, or work, or pottery as activities that assist us in finding out who we are, what our purpose in life is, then the out-of-bounds ball, the product that won't sell, and the broken pot become challenges that provide us with the opportunity to choose the attitude we take in the face of adversity. We choose what stand we take!

THE NINTH HOLE
FRANKL, MEANING, AND GOLF

The human being is driven by the will to meaning. Pleasure and power are secondary and incomplete drives within us. If this is true, how will this change the way we lead and perceive work?

— — — — —

The ninth hole, a 352-yard par 4, is perhaps the easiest hole on the front nine. It's actually drivable when the east wind is blowing. The golfer has the option of going for the green and flying over two demonic pothole bunkers or hitting left, right, or short. The green is large and relatively flat, though it tends to be a bit hard, and rolling off the edge is not uncommon.

Bud approached the ninth tee amazed that he was playing so well despite the profoundly intense conversations he'd had on the last eight holes. Perhaps the deep discussion distracted him from worrying about his game. He saw a dignified elderly man with snow white hair waiting for him on the bench beside the tee. When he met the man's eyes, he saw an individual who had endured a great deal of pain and agony, yet who displayed an aura of dignity and wisdom. Viktor Frankl rose to his feet, gave Bud a warm handshake and smile, and welcomed him to the ninth hole.

Bud. Dr. Frankl, it is a true honour to meet you. I read your first book and it changed my life in many ways.

Frankl. Dear Bud, thank you. It is a pleasure to meet

you as well. I wonder if it was one of your Spitfire flights I heard in 1943 flying over Auschwitz.

Bud. Perhaps. It was a difficult time for all of us in many different ways. It always amazes me how some of us made it through while so many others perished.

Frankl. Yes, of course. As you know, this is the basis of my life's work. While your experience of survival and death was, more often than not, a matter of skilled fighting, what I faced with my comrades was an issue of the skill to live with freedom, responsibility, and meaning.

Bud. It's hard to say which is more difficult - the struggle to survive physically or the struggle to survive philosophically, wouldn't you agree? And you know, while we both faced overpoweringly intense life dramas, it has always struck me that your approach has rarely been used by others to deal with life's more subtle dilemmas.

Frankl. Perhaps. My intent was always to employ my logotherapy with those whose mental illness was related to what I called an existential vacuum or a loss of meaning in life.[10] It was a reactive strategy to depression. In North America, my approach to therapy through meaning has usually been associated by the psychology community with disaster distress or pathology. It has rarely, if ever, been employed as a proactive strategy - particularly in the work context, which I understand is your interest.

Bud. If you would be so kind, I think that we should chat about the subtler forms of logotherapy while we play the ninth.

---

[10] Logotherapy is the name that Frankl gave to his psychological approach. Logos is the Greek word for "meaning," and thus his procedure implies therapy or healing through the search for meaning in life.

Frankl. Capital idea, Bud. Shall I hit first?

Bud. Certainly. I think I'll hit my driver. This hole is far too enticing not to go for the green, and the challenge is what I love about this game.

Frankl. Well, if you are prepared for all possible outcomes then ... fire away.

Bud. What do you plan to hit, Dr. Frankl?

Frankl. I know myself, Bud. Hitting short is the best strategy for me – a drive and 5 iron should do the trick.

Bud hit first. His swing was uncharacteristically fast and his ball landed deep in the first pothole bunker. With a stiff upper lip, he left the tee without saying a word. Frankl hit his driver as well but with a slow methodical swing that floated his ball out about two hundred yards behind the bunker that had swallowed Bud's drive.

Bud. It's been quite a round thus far. I'm not sure I can clearly see the difference anymore between sages and lunatics.

Frankl. Ah, you've played with my colleagues Freud and Adler then, have you?

Bud. Well, yes, but they certainly weren't the only colourful characters I came up against.

Frankl. Yes, yes, it's true, genius and insanity often are close mates, aren't they? But regardless of how bizarre they all seem to be, we can't do without them. I have often said that we need to stand on the shoulders of the past's intellectual giants, no matter how odd or wrong they were, in order to see new horizons in our understanding. For example, let's take Freud and Adler, since I have often used them as foils for my own logotherapy. Freud, as you know from your discussion with him, focussed on the will to pleasure and Adler on the will to power. In both cases, these scholars perceived the individual as seeking some sort of homeostasis, either in terms of the satisfaction of internal drives or instincts, or in terms of overcoming a perceived or real sense of inferiority. The outcome of both of these views is that the individual never strives beyond what biology demands - consciously or subconsciously. Enter Professor Skinner. While he attempts to debunk both of my colleagues' theories with the view that environment is the primary indicator of all behaviour and thoughts, he, like the others, makes what I believe to be the same mistake - the perception that the individual has no free will or responsibility for his or her actions. Freud's human is driven by pleasure, Adler's human is driven by a need to overcome weakness, and Skinner's human is controlled by the environment - nowhere is there choice or responsibility.[11]

Bud. Ah, the existentialist's mantra - freedom and responsibility.

Frankl. Exactly. And while I, of course, do recognize and agree with the existential philosophers, it seems that they have been wonderful at expressing the need to be true to oneself but they say precious little about how to get there. In my career, I wanted to dig deeper and perhaps be more pragmatic in order to expose and use this uniquely human characteristic of freedom and responsibility in my approach to therapy. In other words – free to do what?

---

[11] Existentialists, though a diverse group of thinkers, converge on the idea that the human has free will and that the task of philosophy is to lead the individual toward his or her recognition of this freedom and toward taking responsibility for all outcomes of this capacity to choose.

Frankl arrived at his ball first. He had about 155 yards to the pin and selected a six iron. One smooth swing later, his ball landed hard on the green and rolled off. Bud reached the bunker and found that a ladder was the only way to descend into the sand. Without hope of hitting the green, he took his sand wedge with him and disappeared into the crater. Two shots and he was out on the grass with seventy yards to the pin. With surprising confidence, considering his last few shots, he hit a half wedge and landed ten feet from the pin - bogey in range.

Bud. Tell me, then. Freedom to do what?

Frankl. Freedom to find meaning, Bud, freedom to find meaning. Now, as you have already pointed out, most people associate my name and logotherapy with finding meaning through experiences of profound suffering. We may suffer in more subtle ways as a result of what I have called "existential vacuum." Though this vacuum can result in deep depression and suffering, many go through their lives with a faint yet nagging sense that their lives are not fulfilled. The so-called midlife crisis is the wake-up call we experience when we realize - finally - that what we are doing or have done with our lives has not been by our design, but has been based on what others expect from us. We allow ourselves, through complacency or sheer non-engagement, to live someone else's perception of what we are and what we ought to be doing. We play cricket or football, or become accountants because our parents want us to be athletes or accountants; we seek jobs for pay and security, to purchase things that marketers tell us we need, and so on. Now, we may end up as athletes or accountants and we may be successful, but the question to ask is whether these activities are meaningful to us as individuals separate from our duty and obligation to significant others. The bottom line is that we allow ourselves to be controlled because our own sense of freedom, responsibility, and meaning is hidden or is submerged below the will to pleasure or power. In other words, nature and nurture are the catalysts for our behaviour rather than our authentic freedom to choose. In fact, it's neither nature nor nurture, but something much more human.

Bud. So are you suggesting that we can't find meaning in activities unless we ourselves have chosen them freely?

Frankl. Well, yes and no. Certainly any activity or career will likely be more meaningful if we have carefully selected it from among other options and if it fits with who we think we are. But even when we are stuck in a situation that is not of our choosing - for example, a meeting that we know we should attend despite its probability of excruciating boredom - we still have a chance to find meaning if we choose to engage and contribute. We have the freedom to *choose our attitude* toward the meeting. We may choose in favour of it being a waste of time, and if we do, then our time spent there will be forever lost and meaningless. If, on the other hand, we *choose* to attend and *choose* to be engaged, then although this time will still be irretrievable once it has passed, it will have been time meaningfully spent.[12] It is interesting to sit back and review how many of the events that occur during the average day - even the average holiday - are ones that we could choose to make meaningful if we were aware of the opportunity. These could include a chance to smile at the child next door on her

[12] Heidegger (1962) refers to this in his discussion of beings-unto-death

way to school, or the opportunity to chat with a person from another culture sitting beside you on the train, or exploring the local culture while holidaying at a resort. "Meaning-events" are available to us every day, yet we are oblivious to most of them.

Bud. Dr. Frankl, forgive me, but I think you need to take me back a bit and give me a better idea of what you mean by the word *meaning*.

Frankl. Yes, of course. This is often misunderstood because neither the therapist nor the leader or manager - or parent, for that matter - can tell the other what is meaningful. We can only say that there is meaning to be found, and the task in life for the individual is to discover what is meaningful to him or her. Meaning can be thought of as what gives life purpose, and this can be found in almost anything - whether you're breaking rocks in Calcutta as a form of prayer to Krishna, or conducting an orchestra in Vienna, or managing a firm in Devon. If it fulfills you in some way, then it can be worth doing. This, of course, precludes that which brings harm to others or prevents them from also seeking what is meaningful. In the cases I have given, each activity could also be perceived to be drudgery by another, but the individual has freely chosen the attitude taken in circumstances that may or may not be the individual's doing.

Bud. Okay ... I think. Let's talk about leadership and meaning. But first, you're up.

Frankl walked over to his ball just off the green and, with a 7 iron, chipped up to about fifteen feet of the cup. Bud took out his old familiar Bull's Eye putter and started to line up his putt, and then, unable to concentrate, he straightened up and continued the dialogue.

Bud. I think that maybe I am seeing some connections here with what you have said and with the ideas of the others I have heard today. Before I putt, let me put this to you: leadership is then not necessarily about leading people to where you want them to go but rather about helping them find meaning in what they do. If they can do this within the confines of their jobs, then work becomes a source of meaning - a medium for meaning as opposed a means to some other end, like pleasure, money, or power.

Frankl. Bud, this is the correct application. To seek pleasure or power in the context of work will sooner or later result in the same condition - a sense of meaninglessness and a so-called midlife crisis. To uncover the will to meaning in the people for whom you are responsible is the key to true leadership, in my mind.

Frankl putted and rolled his ball just past the cup - a tap-in bogey. Bud returned to his stance, surveyed his putt, and, with far too much going on in his mind, effortlessly stroked the ball into the cup - bogey. The men walked off the ninth green and decided to sit and chat for a few more minutes.

Bud. So the leader creates an environment in which each individual is encouraged and supported to open up to the possibility of meaningful work … sounds a lot like Martin Heidegger.

Frankl. Well, no great surprise, as Martin is a very dear friend of mine and had a great deal of influence on my thinking, as did many of the other existential philosophers.

Bud. I am also thinking of Socrates at the moment - how better to uncover hidden meaning than through a philosophical midwife.

Frankl. The dots seem to be connecting for you.

Bud. I feel somewhat overwhelmed and calm at the same time. I need to consider all that has happened in the last two hours. I think I'll head back to the clubhouse and try to put all of this into perspective.

Frankl. Bud, I think that is a wise decision. While these ideas are fresh, chase after them – the golf course will always be here.

With that, Bud grabbed his clubs and started walking back to the clubhouse. How was he to make sense of all of this? How would he put it into practice?

Relevance of Frankl

Our search for meaning, Frankl argues, is our primary motivator. This is a difficult concept to grasp for the baby-boomer and post–baby-boomer generations, since we have typically understood that a meaningful life, and specifically meaningful work, are to be secondary, or somehow wrapped into the more vital objectives of salary, security, and weekends spent forgetting about the office. While Frankl acknowledges that there are other drives that influence our behaviour (for example, the will to pleasure and the will to power, as identified by his peers Freud and Adler, respectively), he suggests that our need to make sense of and find meaning in life is fundamental to the human being, whether we know it or not. Furthermore, meaning can be achieved through our work, in addition to our experiences and relationships and our attitude toward suffering. This notion rarely enters the mind of the organisational leader whose job it is to ensure efficient and productive output from employees toward preset organisational goals. Whether the worker is experiencing meaningful work is irrelevant. However, some progressive, or at least more innovative, attempts have been made to align workplace values and goals with personal values and goals. This is done in order for the employee to identify with the organisation – to be part of the "family," but it is more often than not a veiled attempt to appeal to a deeper sense of obligation in order to obtain a higher level of motivation and output. Whether one is part of a neo-Taylorian workplace (McDonalds, for example) or a "family" with its overt and subtle pressure to conform, the ultimate end is in fact the bottom line, not meaning.

The Logos-leader (that is, a meaning-leader) leader would see work as a medium through which meaning can be found. Profit and efficiency, while not undesirable, would come about as secondary outcomes. The psychological parallel to the will to pleasure and power is self-evident. The Logos-leader would not be a laissez-faire "hippy" who would allow anything to occur, "as long as it has meaning for you, dude." Rather, the work would get done and done well, but at the same time, the employees would be skilled in critically reflecting upon their own reasons for working. They would be profoundly aware of the impact that their efforts were having on those around them, as well as on those they served.

If meaning is the primary will, then it stands to reason that the key to leadership is to help employees to uncover what it is that is meaningful to them and how this may dovetail with their working life - regardless what their tasks might be. It is here that Frankl and Socrates connect, as the latter does not dictate truth but asks appropriate questions to uncover it. The leader, then, cannot tell the followers what is meaningful but needs to help them to discover for themselves what provides meaning. Work becomes a vehicle through which each one of us can participate in what we perceive to be meaningful. Let's consider the following hypothetical example in healthcare:

> Nurse A supervises a team of nurses in an extended care home and views his job and those of his staff as a means to pay the bills. Neither he nor his staff find much meaning in their day-to-day activities, and they generally see themselves as merely role-occupants. This institution is prudent with its resources and commands an efficient and effective style of management and patient care in logical batch processes – individual needs are inefficient hindrances to the "machine."
>
> Nurse B is a leader in a different type of seniors' home. While she acknowledges that the work has to be done and that systems have to be in place, she ensures that each and every member of her staff is first and foremost aware of why they have chosen to be in the nursing profession, why they have agreed to work in a seniors' home, and what specific challenges they will face in caring for this particular population. For example, the notion of loss of personhood among seniors with dementia is cause for a variety of staff behaviours, from reluctance to treat pain adequately to the use of restraint and even ridicule and abuse. It also gives rise to the potential for deep introspection regarding what exactly a person is and the nature of ethical and meaningful relationship and caring. The outcome is that Nurse B and her staff have attempted to understand what motivates them meaningfully and how the context in which they find themselves helps them to achieve a greater sense of meaning in their lives.

As leaders, our job is not always about enhancing or improving the organisation or helping it to become more efficient. A major part of effective leadership remains in the affective realm of helping employees to find meaning in their roles and practices. This means helping to connect or reconnect the concepts of occupation, compassion, and agency. Consequently, effective leadership is about the humanistic and tacit aspects that are fundamentally located in the relational.

The Driving Range: Putting Theory into Practice

So what is Frankl getting at here? If we believed that meaning is the primary drive, how differently would we act? Would we structure our organisations so that meaning was the primary incentive as opposed to money, status, and security? Would our approach to leadership change? Would our expectations of leaders change and thus would the training and education that our leaders receive have a different focus?

...Off to the Clubhouse.

The Clubhouse

As Bud walked off the ninth green to the clubhouse for a sandwich and cool lemonade, he wondered how he was going to put all of this together – how was this going to change his own leadership style? Typically he would have already been assessing his play on the front nine – adding up his putts missed - but this time golf was very much a secondary concern. He felt as though he had been given pieces of the *leadership puzzle* from some of the world's greatest thinkers and needed badly to put them together to see the big picture not unlike the meditative thinking that Heidegger talked to him about on the third hole. Was there a big picture at all? Were these nine separate and distinct conversations that would take him off in nine or more different directions? He grabbed his lunch and walked over to his usual spot with a view of the 18th green. No great surprise that everyone from Socrates to Frankl were already there waiting for him. A bit shocked at the sight of them - he felt as if he was about to experience some sort of grand test to see if he had grasped the knowledge they had gifted to him. Socrates, naturally, was the first to speak.

Socrates: My dear Bud. What a day you have had. One never knows who you will meet on a golf course and what conversations you will have – dead philosophers coming alive would not have been your first guess this morning as you rolled out of bed! As you know my trademark is not to answer questions but to ask them. So, I have three for you. Let's see where they take you in your quest.

- What are we?

- How should we live?
- What should we do?

Now, these are not new questions; in fact I spent my life in pursuit of them and they continue to be the basic questions that any student of philosophy should and does consider. Let's narrow them a bit more to reflect our conversations today:

- What are we as leaders and followers?
- How should we live as leaders?
- What should I do as a leader?

What are we as leaders and followers?

Bud: Ok, here goes!

Freud, Adler, Skinner, and Sartre gave me unique insights into this most basic assumption. What we think we are, or what the other person is, sets the foundation for how we will lead or follow. Drs. Freud and Adler argue that the individual is shaped by instincts and believed that behaviour is the outcome of one's efforts to fulfill or avoid the drives to pleasure or power. In essence, individuals are involved in an internal and subconscious battle with nature, and these drives define behaviour. Skinner provided me with a somewhat similar view of the person insofar as we are defined by something external to us. In Skinner's world, we are the products of our environment. That is, we are the result of our internalization of positive or negative reinforcement to external stimuli – today we eat our peas because as children we received dessert if we did and we work hard in our jobs with the expectation we will be paid. So what are we according to the likes of Freud, Adler, and Skinner? We are the result of natural drives and/or our environment; this implies that free will is not involved and thus little or no acknowledgement of responsibility can justifiably be expected. In other words, whatever I do - good or bad - is not my fault and I am not in control nor am I responsible.

If this is true, then leadership will focus on controlling the environment - its workflow and reward structure in order to mould individual behaviour into what the organisation needs. Not only is the authentic individual irrelevant - it does not exist. The world according to Sartre could not be more different. He believes that we are condemned to be free and must suffer the agony (or joy) of this capacity to choose. He suggests that we are not pawns of biological drives or of societal or organisational expectations. Instead, we are free and thus have the capacity to make ourselves who we are. Followers, then, are individuals perceived to be in the process of becoming who they choose to be, and leaders are, as Professor Heidegger suggested, to "leap ahead" and clear the path for their self-awareness through their work experiences as opposed to "leap in" and control behaviour.

I guess the problem I have with Professors Skinner, Adler, and Freud is that if they are correct, then as an individual I might as well stop my quest here and now as I have no real control going forward. Either my drives or my environment have already chosen the path and I am subconsciously along for the ride. If on the other hand, as the rest of you have stated directly or indirectly, I have some degree of freedom to chose a path, then I can act - well or badly - but most importantly I have the capacity to choose, change, develop, grow as do those who "follow" me.

Ask Yourself:

I. To what extent am I *free* to choose my work-related course of action? While I recognise there are certain things I must do as part of my contractual obligation, what degrees of freedom/choice do I have?

II. What amount of 'freedom' is acceptable for my employees? What are their boundaries? Do they recognise this 'space' as freedom? Do they recognise their freedom and responsibility?

III. To what extent do I see my role as a facilitator of work-related meaning or someone who gets things done?

IV. Do I leap-ahead and help them self-discover or leap-in and direct behaviour? When should I do one or the other?

How should we live as leaders?

On the second and fourth holes, I played with Aristotle and Nietzsche, who provided me with two very different perspectives of how anyone of us should live our life. Aristotle suggested that the purpose of life is to flourish, and to do so, one must live virtuously (and have a modicum of good luck, or one's fair share of lucky bounces off trees into the fairway). Virtue, the mean between excess and deficit, is to be considered in every choice we make, from socializing with clients, to

fitness, to maintaining good health, to choosing the right club on the golf course. The leader's role, then, is to facilitate this notion of virtue through role modelling, decisions, policies, communication, and education in order to direct individuals and organisations toward their potential. The leader's role is also to help others recognise the difference between real and apparent good. The former enhances the "soul" (of the individual or the organisation); the latter will, sooner or later, destroy it.

Nietzsche was equally concerned about the idea of flourishing/self-actualisation but called it the will to power. He believed that it was incumbent on each individual to strive beyond the mediocre, the average, and to extend beyond what society expected or perhaps accepted. Thus the Nietzschean leader will attempt to awaken a sense of passion in the individual and will use work as a medium through which individual potential can be realized. The follower, Nietzsche believed, is susceptible to the pressure of the crowd to be average and mediocre. The role of the leader, therefore, is to jolt followers out of their complacency so they can achieve personal greatness. One's life as a leader, then, should be spent in a constant attempt to foster virtue and the passion to flourish within oneself, those whom one leads, and one's organisation.

Ask yourself:

I. Am I on a path to reach my potential as a leader (or am I stuck in the minutia of *everydayness* and can't get to vision)?

II. When I make decisions, are they virtue-based (real good) or expediency-based (apparent good) (i.e., are they contributing to the wellness of my leadership "soul'? To the organisation's 'soul').

III. What kind of behaviour am I fostering among my employees - real or apparent good? Specifically what do I do and say to them to encourage virtuous behaviour?

What should you do as a leader?

To answer this question, I want to reflect on what I was told by Heidegger, Socrates, and Vivekananda. Heidegger revealed to me that we know what we know and do what we do today because of our overemphasis on *calculative thinking*. As a consequence of this emphasis, we have forgotten our ability to think meditatively or reflectively. We don't see the big picture (like leadership) anymore because of our intense grip on the throat of technology-as-reality to the exclusion of deeper philosophical work.

Much of how we understand the functions of the leader is the result of this sort of thinking. Where the values of efficiency, effectiveness, and productivity run the show, there is precious little time or reward for the kind of meditative thinking that Heidegger argued we should be doing in addition to the nuts and bolts of calculative leadership. I took this to be a call for a broader vision of the consequences of leadership. It is not so much about getting the job done as it is about ensuring that employees know why the job should be done and that individuals are experiencing meaning as a function of the job.

In a somewhat similar vein, Vivekananda suggests that we mistakenly focus our thinking exclusively on the outcome/goal - the result of our intense desire for linear evaluation - and thus we fail to pay primary attention to the process. Because our concentration on process is so superficial, the basis for our knowledge about the world has become narrowly focussed on winning or losing, success or failure. If the task itself can be perceived to be of primary importance, the consequences will come - it's a simple matter of cause and effect. The leader's efforts, then, need to be redirected to the process of work so that work in itself becomes valued rather than just the outcome.

When Socrates joined me this morning, our conversation focussed on the idea of giving birth to ideas: the leader's role is to facilitate the arrival of these new-born concepts, plans, strategies, proposals, and solutions. In our context of work and leadership, the essence of this message is that employees have perspectives of their own. If the thinking leader is open to working with people, then the possibilities and potential for growth become staggering. With such an approach to leadership, one that is truly collaborative and inclusive, everyone becomes engaged and empowered to create. The process of inquiry-based teamwork thrives. Inquiry means the ability to draw connections between theories and particular experiences and realities, to converse meaningfully with others, and to begin to build a comprehensible understanding and demonstration of practice. This is what teamwork should be based on because all talents, experiences, and modes of practice can come together in a meaningful way that encourages creative solutions to difficult problems. In reality, the employees are often closer (physically and cognitively) to dilemmas than the managers/administrators who oversee their work; the employees therefore know better how to resolve problems or design innovations. The leader, then, must recognise and have faith in the ability and willingness of the follower to participate in defining and resolving problems within the organization. Leadership needs to be encouraged among everyone who works in the organization - not just bosses, but leaders who enable others through a supportive workplace community of practice.

This makes me think of the following examples:

i. A child returns from a football match event and reports to the parent that her team won: thus ends the conversation.

ii. A salesperson reports to the boss that a major

> contract has been secured, never revealing the details. The boss doesn't ask – ignorance about process is bliss.

These are not unusual examples, nor are they unusual responses by the parent or the boss. However, having played the last nine holes with the likes of these philosophers, in true Socratic fashion, a leader might ask pointed questions to allow the meaning of the situation to be 'self-revealed".

> Example i. Winning is great but how did she play? Why did she feel the victory was important? What about her performance was she proud of? What could she have done differently? What does she need to improve? How can I help? And…what did she "get" from the victory? What knowledge will she take forward to the next practice, the next game? What did she learn about herself as a person?

> Example ii. What are the details surrounding this contract? What did we have to do to 'seal the deal'? What were the pressures to sign? If we made the details public, are they defendable? Did our process align with the company's ethics code/policy? Are you proud of the way you approached this contract? Did you feel you acted in "good faith" and had 'real vs. apparent" good in mind? Is this deal consistent with the company's vision and values?

These are just a few examples, but you get the point. We get so caught up in the everyday-ness of our busy lives that we forget why we do what we do and miss the opportunity to connect our work – our successes and failures- with a broader understanding of who we are as beings that naturally seek meaning. So let's consider this further.

First, the leader entertains the possibility that a follower has something to say - pregnant with ideas. Second, the leader realises that the immediate win or sale is not the focus of participation in the organisation. Rather, the real intent of organisational membership is the long-term involvement in virtuous work that results in process-based success over time, personally and organisationally.

Then there was you, Viktor Frankl, on the final hole. I had read your book, *Man's Search for Meaning* in university and I always thought it was left unfortunately to obscurity in practice, though known in general for the dramatic story of your time in Nazi death camps. Dr. Frankl you might well be the missing link in the often mundane world of work. Your system, logotherapy (that is, therapy or healing through meaning), is based upon the premise that meaning can be found in all things - from the desperation of the death camp to a well played par 5. You designed logotherapy to overcome what you called an existential vacuum: the condition of angst that results when meaning cannot be found in life - it may be lost, latent, or altogether unknown. Logotherapy for the depressed is, of course, an interesting and often effective strategy, but is the diagnosis of depression the only starting point from which the pursuit of meaning can arise? Is this concern for meaning necessarily a reactive search stemming from despair or can it be a proactive component of leadership?

You said that meaning cannot be imposed, in the same way as one cannot be forced to laugh or love. But can meaning be facilitated? Can a leader create an environment through which an organisational member can find his or her own sense of life's purpose?

Ask yourself:

I. What do I do as a leader? How would you describe your typical week? What amount of time is spent on task-oriented activity? What time is spent thinking strategically? What time is spent fostering meaning within the organisation? For oneself? For employees?

II. What would the ideal workweek look like? What kind of behaviour would you expect from yourself and from your employees in this ideal week? If you are not there…what do you need to do to move closer to this ideal?

III. Do you have a sense of an ultimate goal for leadership? If you were to write your own leadership epitaph, what would you want it to say? How would you want your children to describe your leadership? If you are not doing this now, what do you need to change?

The Dead Philosopher-golfers nodded their heads in approval, with the exception of Skinner, Adler, and Freud, of course. They could not get their heads around the notion of free will or virtue. It may well be a leap of faith to disagree with them and believe that each individual has the capacity for decisions, for change, and to select a path to leadership and followership that is authentic.

...Bud wakes up. Head throbbing and sees his son kneeling over him with an exceptionally worried look on his face. Brian helps him to his feet and they make their way back to the locker room to find some ice for golf ball sized lump on Bud's forehead. He was unconscious for seconds but the conversations in his head were as clear as if they had happened. Dave and Don were in the locker room when they came in out of the rain and Bud told his bizarre story.

For Bud, the opportunity for learning resulted from a painful mishap on the golf course; we hope that reading through this short text has been a less painful but equally enlightening experience for you. Opportunity and synchronicity knock at strange times, and it is our hope that this book finds you at a time in your life or career when you need another perspective to help solve the dilemmas you are facing. Nine perspectives have been presented, and each offers you something to ponder, perhaps internalize, or even outright reject. But if we have you thinking about meaning and about creating an environment for others to find meaning, our mission has been accomplished and the three of us can meet at the tee and see if we can put any of this into action ourselves … keep your head down!

Appendix A

Overview: Philosophers on Leadership

Socrates & Leadership: Leadership is midwifery. Pull what you can from the individual's mind by asking questions. In this way, individuals become aware of their own abilities to be engaged and to take pride in their work.

Aristotle & Leadership: The goal of living is to flourish and we can do this through work if it is balanced. Balance implies that one of the objectives of work is to develop a deeper understanding of oneself. The leader's role is to ensure that this potential for self-discovery can be found in each person's organisational role - regardless of what it is.

Heidegger & Leadership: To fully understand any decision we make, we must be able to think both calculatively and meditatively. Leaders must know the "why" as well as the "what" and the "how."

Nietzsche & Leadership: Self-awareness can only come about when one pushes the limits of one's ability. Pain is not to be avoided but to be welcomed in the same way that a well-exercised muscle must break down before it can be made stronger.

Vivekananda & Leadership: Attachment leads to misplaced desire, and misplaced desire leads to suffering. Work can be seen as more than what it is - we need to demand more from it. Leaders need to understand this and to begin to fulfill their primary obligation.

Sartre & Leadership: We're in flight from responsibility. Leaders, in the same manner as good parents, need to create an environment in which free will is acknowledged and responsibility for all behaviour is recognized. A policy has never made a decision - this is a human endeavour.

Freud and Adler & Leadership: It is a given that pleasure and/or power are what make us tick in life, and in organisations, we are controlled by the need to satisfy drives and to overcome what we lack. The organisation thrives on this knowledge.

Skinner & Leadership: Free will is either wishful thinking or a potential curse on the organisation. Organisations depend on human programming - otherwise why would we accept meaningless toil as the dominant feature of our lives?

Frankl & Leadership: The human being is driven by the will to meaning. Pleasure and power are secondary and incomplete drives in us. If we accept this as true, how will we lead others and perceive work differently?

Appendix B
Biographies of Our Golfers
In Order of Appearance

Socrates (470–399 BCE)

Socrates, the father of Western philosophy, was a citizen of Athens during the height of its intellectual, political, and artistic glory. While other philosophers were certainly active during and before the fifth century BCE, none have left as lasting an impression as this man. He actually wrote nothing. Most of what we know about him and his philosophy, we gather from Plato, who was one of his pupils. Plato chose to use Socrates as the main character for most of the dialogues he wrote to express his own perspectives on philosophy. Thus, one can never be sure of what can be attributed to Socrates and what is Plato's. Regardless, he likely existed and died for his refusal to back away from his philosophy. While so many of the dialogues Plato wrote are of direct or indirect relevance to our topic at hand, we would like to point the reader to the *Phaedrus* and the *Symposium*. On the surface, these dialogues concern his views of love and beauty, but on deeper reflection, they are directed to our perception of the other, which has been a theme through this book.

Aristotle (384–322 BCE)

Aristotle was a pupil of Plato, the son of Phillip of Macedon's physician, and the tutor of Alexander the Great. Though Aristotle studied under Plato, he had a very different idea of the way philosophy worked. While Socrates and Plato were both deeply committed to idealism, Aristotle was firmly a realist. Look at Raphael's sixteenth-century painting *The School of Athens* and you will see Plato and Aristotle walking side by side, Plato with his finger pointing to the heavens (idealism) and Aristotle motioning downward to the ground (realism). While Aristotle had a great deal to say about many different topics, from metaphysics to reproduction to poetry, for our purposes, his *Nichomachean Ethics* is the most salient; here he writes about virtue and the goal of living (and working) – *eudaimonia*.

Martin Heidegger (1884–1976)

Martin Heidegger was a German existentialist of the twentieth century. Although his work has been overshadowed by his involvement with the Nazi party prior to the Second World War, it is known by philosophy students to be deeply insightful but almost impenetrable. Having said that, his *Memorial Address* (in his *Discourse on Thinking*), in which he discusses at length the notions of calculative and meditative thinking, is rather an easy read, as Heidegger goes.

Friedrich Nietzsche (1844–1900)

Friedrich Nietzsche is one of the most bizarre characters on our golf course. His primary thrust in philosophy was the will to power, yet he himself never possessed any of it – other than a powerful mind that was more or less ignored until many years after his death. Nietzsche suffered from ill health all of his life and lasted only a short time as a professor due to his physical ailments. Despite this, he wrote prolifically and offered the Western world a profound counterpoint to the mainstream philosophical writings of Mill, Kant, and

Hegel. He was an existentialist, though he sided strongly with naturalism, believing that the primary human drive is to seek power as an individual. Though his thinking did change substantially through his life as a scholar, his initial work, *The Birth of Tragedy,* is the best example of his belief in the Apollinian-Dionysian aspect of the human's essence.

Swami Vivekananda (1863–1902)

Swami Vivekananda, born into an aristocratic family in Calcutta, was a dedicated student of Western philosophy as a young man. Devoted to the mystic Sri Ramakrishna, he became one of India's most influential spiritual leaders in the late nineteenth century. Vivekananda became well known in the West following his famous lecture tours in the United States and the United Kingdom, in which he not only presented the West with a coherent account of Hinduism but also emphasized the necessity of building a harmonious relationship between Western materialism and Hindu spirituality. His ideas are clearly influenced by the *Bhagavad-Gita,* which preceded Martin Heidegger's notion of calculative and meditative thinking by almost two thousand years.

Jean-Paul Sartre (1905–80)

Jean-Paul Sartre was a philosopher, playwright, and World War II underground resistance fighter. When one thinks of existential philosophy, this beret-wearing, Gitane-smoking Frenchman in a Paris café comes to mind. His most famous work, *Being and Nothingness,* is ground zero for the philosophy that espouses freedom and responsibility. The shorter and more reader-friendly

Existentialism and Human Emotions is also a must read for anyone who wishes to gain further insight into existentialism. His plays are deeply insightful and, like the dialogues of Plato, actually make philosophy enjoyable with the banter between characters about life and the ontology of freedom. When Sartre died in 1980, his funeral was attended by more than fifty thousand mourners – a far cry from the Athenians' execution of their philosophical son, Socrates.

Sigmund Freud (1856–1939)

Freud's background and studies in neurology and psychiatry eventually led him to view the human organism as a system of drives common to other organisms, forever paying homage to Darwin – in his words, "the great Darwin." Preoccupation with drives led him to formulate the intricate balance of the id, ego, and superego, with sexual drive being the dominant force. Freud used the term *libido* to refer to total psychic energy, and over the years, with his insistence on the primacy of the sexual drive, *libido* became synonymous with that drive. He viewed dreams as the road to the unconscious, the storehouse of defence-mechanism development, especially repression. He is generally acknowledged as the father of psychoanalysis.

Hitler's Germany forced Freud to leave for England, where, after a fifteen-year battle, he died of cancer of the mouth. As if that tormented death was not enough, he had to endure the wholesale burning of his works, although his son Martin managed to get some of them to Switzerland before they could be purged. Freud's daughter Anna was held by the Gestapo concerning her membership in the International Psychoanalytic Association.

The best single sources for Freud and his works are biographies such as P. Gay's *Freud: A Life for Our Time*.

Alfred Adler (1870–1937)

Adler was born to a well-to-do household, the third of five boys and two girls. All the children were gifted in music, especially Alfred, who had a beautiful tenor voice. His mother was cold, nervous, and gloomy in disposition, whereas his father was happy and strong-willed, and insisted that his children have great personal freedom, but he never punished nor caressed them. Adler was a mediocre student who was terrified of math, but he eventually succeeded in medical school and later aligned himself with Sigmund Freud and Carl Gustav Jung, forming the trinity of psychoanalysis.

Adler's primary contributions to understanding human behaviour centre on his development of individual psychology; the striving for perfection or will to power, which is a consequence of our inherent inferiority complexes; and concern for the betterment of society, which he called social interest. His thinking was heavily influenced by the German philosopher Hans Vaihinger and Vaihinger's *Philosophy of As-If*, where "fictions" are the real determinants of how we react to environmental influences.

The best source for those interested in Adlerian psychology is Adler's classic text entitled, Individual Psychology (1964) published by Harper Perennial.

B.F. Skinner (1904–90)

Burrhus Frederic (B.F.) Skinner is acknowledged as one of America's foremost psychologists, having published some twenty-one books and more than 180 professional articles. It was Bertrand Russell's thinking about society's poor prospects for a better future and the ideas of John B. Watson that turned Skinner to psychology, a field of study that he believed had to be rooted in science. And it was the scientific approach that led him to develop the now familiar ideas on conditioning and reinforcement schedules, which pervade virtually all milieus, especially that of the workplace.

Skinner's two greatest books, *Walden Two* and *Beyond Freedom and Dignity*, polarized social science thinkers, placing them in two camps: those who supported his views that humans are not autonomous beings and those who adhered to the belief that humans have some kind of innate mechanism, often referred to as free will, that is tied directly to individuals being responsible for their own behaviour. For Skinner, ever the scientist, the thinking of the latter group had to be replaced by a deeper understanding of how environment conditions our behaviour. Later in life (1987), he acknowledged that behaviourism was being overshadowed by the re-emergence of humanistic philosophy, psychotherapy, and cognitive psychology. –

Viktor E. Frankl (1905–97)

Viktor E. Frankl has clearly played a major role in the development of this book. His ideas are increasingly relevant to us in the twenty-first century as we deal with ever grander scales of war, technological change, and the decay and transformation of cultures and traditions. Frankl was born in Vienna and was a psychiatrist and neurologist prior to World War II. He was interned in Nazi death camps from 1942 until the end of the war. While he had envisioned aspects of logotherapy prior to his experience in the camps, his ideas were not formally published until 1946 with the first edition of *Man's Search for Meaning*. His notions of existential vacuum, existential anxiety, and hardiness have been the subjects of numerous studies involving soldiers, nurses, students, and so on.

Bibliography

Adler, A. 1963. *Understanding Human Nature*. Trans. Walter Brian Wolfe. Greenwich, CT: Fawcett. (Orig. pub. 1927.)

Ansbacher, H. L., & Ansbacher, R. (1956). *The individual psychology of Alfred Adler:*

A systematic presentation in selections from his writings. Oxford England: Basic Books.

Aristotle. 1992. *Nichomachean Ethics*. Trans. W.D. Ross. In *The Basic Works of Aristotle,* ed. R. McKeon, 935–1126. New York: Random House.

Burns, J.M. (1978). *Leadership*. New York: Harper & Row.

Crumbaugh, J.C. 1988. *Everything to Gain*. Berkeley: Institute of Logotherapy Press.

Frankl, V. 1988. *The Will to Meaning*. New York: Meridian Books.

Frankl, V. 2006. *Man's Search for Meaning*. Trans. I. Lasch. Boston: Beacon Press. (Orig. pub. 1959.)

Freud, S. 1974. *The Future of an Illusion*. Vol. 21 of *Collected Works of Sigmund Freud,* eds. James Strachey and Anna Freud. London: Hogarth Press. (Orig. pub. 1927.)

Freud, S. *Civilization and Its Discontents*.

Gay, P. 1988. *Freud: A Life for Our Time*. New York: Norton.

Heiddeger, M. *Being and Time*. Oxford: Blackwell. (Orig. pub. 1927.)

Heidegger, M. 1966. *Discourse on Thinking*. New York: Harper & Row.

Hodgkinson, C. 1983. *Philosophy of Leadership*. Oxford: Basil Blackwell.

Hodgkinson, C. 1996. *Administrative Philosophy*. New York: Pergamon.

Lang, D.L., and D.C. Malloy. 2006. *Leadership: The Final Cause of Good and Evil*. Leeds, UK: Wisdom House.

Malloy, D.C., T., Hadjistavropoulos, E. Fahey McCarthy, D.H. Zakus, I. Park, Y. Lee, J. Williamson, 2009. Culture, Organisational Climate and Ontology: An International Study of Nurses' Insights into their Relationship with Physicians. *Nursing Ethics, 16(6)*, 719-733.

Nietzsche, F. 1992. *Beyond Good and Evil*. In *Basic Writings of Nietzsche*, ed. and trans. W. Kaufman, 179–436. New York: The Modern Library.

Nietzsche, F. 1992. *The Birth of Tragedy*. In *Basic Writings of Nietzsche*, ed. and trans. W. Kaufman, 1-144. New York: The Modern Library.

Pattakos, A. 2004. *Prisoners of Our Thoughts*. San Francisco: Berrett-Koehler.

Plato. 1956. *Phaedrus*. Trans. W.C. Helmbold and W.G. Rabinowitz. New York: Macmillan.

Plato. 1956. *Symposium*. Trans. J.C.G. Rouse. In *Great Dialogues of Plato*, 69–117. New York: Signet.

Sartre, J. 1957. *Existentialism and Human Emotions*. New York: The Winston Library.

Sartre, J. 1989. *The Flies*. In No Exit *and Three Other Plays*, 47–124. New York: Vintage International.

Sartre, J. 1993. *Being and Nothingness*. New York: Washington Square Press.

Sartre, J. 1998. *Existentialism and Human Emotions*. Toronto: Canadian Manda Group. (Orig. pub. 1957.)

Shaw, W.H., and V. Barry. 1989. *Moral Issues in Business*. Belmont: Wadsworth.

Skinner, B.F. 1962. *Walden Two*. New York: Macmillan.

Skinner, B.F. 1971. *Beyond Freedom and Dignity*. New York: Bantam.

Skinner, B.F. 1987. *Whatever Happened To Psychology As A Science Of Behaviour?* American Psychologist, 780-786.

Vivekananda. 1999. "Work and Its Secret." Calcutta: Advaita Ashrama.

About the Authors

Dr. David Cruise Malloy is currently the Vice President-Research University of Regina, Canada. He is a Professor of Applied Philosophy, the Principal Investigator of the International Healthcare Ethics Research Team, and the Honorary Director of the Research Institute for Multiculturalism and Applied Philosophy at Hunan University in China. He is a Fellow of the American Philosophical Practitioners Association. Dr. Malloy is a federally funded ethics researcher in Canada and the author of four texts in applied philosophy, numerous scholarly publications and international conference presentations. His father was a decorated Spitfire fighter pilot in WWII and retired from the military to become a first rate golf professional. David plays golf infrequently and badly, though he holds out hope for his daughters.

Dr. Donald Lyle Lang, Lieutenant-Commander (Ret'd) PhD, was with Canada's military for thirty-one years as an applied psychologist. He currently lectures in leadership, management, organizational psychology, and research methods at the University of Victoria, Canada. His principal research areas: organizational commitment, values, ethics and a critical analysis of good and evil.

CPSIA information can be obtained
at www.ICGtesting.com
Printed in the USA
LVOW08s1509191216
517951LV00001B/51/P